C000017647

MODERN CHAKRAS

VERDA HARPER

CONTENTS

Part II

UNDERSTANDING THE
TECHNIQUES USED TO BALANCE
CHAKRAS

Part III
A STEP-BY-STEP GUIDE TO BALANCING CHAKRAS

© **Copyright Wryting Ltd 2020 - All rights reserved.**

The content contained within this book may not be reproduced, duplicated or transmitted without direct written permission from the author or the publisher.

Under no circumstances will any blame or legal responsibility be held against the publisher, or author, for any damages, reparation, or monetary loss due to the information contained within this book, either directly or indirectly.

Legal Notice:

This book is copyright protected. It is only for personal use. You cannot amend, distribute, sell, use, quote or paraphrase any part, or the content within this book, without the consent of the author or publisher.

Disclaimer Notice:

Please note the information contained within this document is for educational and entertainment purposes only. All effort has been executed to present accurate, up to date, reliable, complete information. No warranties of any kind are declared or implied. Readers acknowledge that the author is not engaged in the rendering of legal, financial, medical or professional advice. The content within this book has been derived from various sources. Please consult a licensed professional before attempting any techniques outlined in this book.

By reading this document, the reader agrees that under no circumstances is the author responsible for any losses, direct or indirect, that are incurred as a result of the use of the information contained within this document, including, but not limited to, errors, omissions, or inaccuracies.

10 WAYS TO PREPARE
FOR THE SUCCESSFUL USE OF
HEALING WITH
MANTRAS AND CHAKRAS

This checklist includes:

- 10 ways to prepare for the successful use of healing with Mantras and Chakras.
- The highest quality items.
- Where you can buy these items for the lowest price.

The last thing we want is for your healing start to be delayed because you weren't as prepared as you could be.

To receive your checklist, visit the link:

INTRODUCTION

It seems like a lifetime ago now but towards my late 20s, I fell into a bit of a slump that I couldn't get out of. It shouldn't have been that way because life was good but there was something out of place that I couldn't label or identify.

If you have read my book Healing Mantras, you will remember my rather individual friend who passionately threw herself into spiritualism. She was somewhat misguided and felt the need to keep putting her crystals on various parts of my body while she chanted. I didn't feel like I was being healed at all, in fact, I felt quite uncomfortable really.

I couldn't tell her this. She was completely convinced that she had become a spiritual healer. I thought I should find some proof that she was being conned. And so, my research began. The first book I read on Chakras and their healing potential was like listening to the juiciest piece of gossip. Talking to myself I filled the room with "No Way!!", "Really!!", and endless "Seriously"s. I learnt that although my friend's methods were wrong, I soon realised that understanding chakras could provide me with the help I needed.

"When you touch the celestial in your heart, you will realise that the beauty of your soul is so pure, so vast and so devastating that you have no option but to merge with it. You have no other option but to feel the rhythm of the universe in the rhythm of your heart."

— AMIT RAY

I came across this quote and I felt it made great sense. Each and every one of us has so much power and potential but it is rare that we are able to use this.

We can't reach our potential because, on the one hand, we are lost by what this is. We might focus on our potential with our day to day responsibilities, whether at work or at home. We can see our potential in a hobby or a sport. But what about our potential to be a good human being? To pick up someone else's trash or to spend some time with the old neighbour because she has no family.

On the other hand, there is already so much weight on our shoulders, can we really take on anymore? Feeling the true beauty of your heart is so impactful and awakening that we may fear this. There is too much to cope with already and you can't pull yourself away from what society tells us is important.

In today's world, it is impossible to escape stress. We live under so much pressure to be the best at everything we do and to be successful, we spend almost all of our time reaching for success but when we get there, we always want more. For some, it is just impossible to break free from the pressure they are under to accomplish even the smallest of things.

This has massive health impacts, both physically and mentally. Chronic stress can lead to negative behaviours like alcohol abuse and overeating for example. Emotionally, we feel anxious and even depressed.

Others may have suffered traumatic times in their past, an abusive partner, divorce, or the loss of someone close to them. Such events are incredibly difficult to move on from and some-times without help, people can never start appreciating life again.

At the same time, your life could be going relatively well, but you still feel like something is out of place, that there is an imbalance in your life and if you knew how to correct this, you feel that you would be able to find some inner peace, perhaps even enjoy the beauty in the world rather than letting the negatives overpower you.

Your interest in chakras might be similar to mine at first, pure curiosity. You might have a physical or mental illness that you feel will benefit from unblocking your chakras, or that you are desperately looking for a way to find some mental peace. Even if you want to learn about chakras so that you can help others, we are going to delve deep into the world of chakras and how they can be used in our modern world.

Together, we will work through techniques on how to unblock your chakras so that you can take advantage of the energy that is kept within us. It is important for me to provide as many tools as possible so that you can experiment and see which methods best suit you, so feel free to use the ideas that, to an extent, get you excited and motivated. The aim is not to make this a lecture with daily homework.

The results can be life-changing, and I don't want to sound dramatic here. Since studying chakras, how they are used, and their specific benefits, I have seen not only improvements in my life but also in all of those that I have worked with- even the complete sceptics.

We have learnt how to take care of ourselves so that we are better able to help others. We have found more motivation to do things that we often put off, whether that's the spring cleaning or the cruise we always dreamed of. By unblocking our chakras, we have been able to find happiness in our lives and to really feel the rhythm of our hearts.

I changed my life from one of going through the motions to one of significance. I knew I didn't want just to be someone's wife or someone's mum. I wanted to continue with my roles but define myself as more. By creating balance in my life, I found the confidence to not only meet like-minded people but also to share my learnings and my zest with others.

My journey started with one of doubt and I admit I was dubious of this Eastern philosophy. The more I discovered, the hungrier I became for the subject. I collaborated with medical practitioners, physiotherapists, and psychologists as well as spiritual experts in order to gain an extensive understanding of chakras. I became so passionate about chakras that I wanted to know everything there was to know, starting with the foundations of chakras.

PART I
THE WHAT, WHERE AND WHY OF CHAKRAS

In the first part of this book, we are going to gain a fundamental knowledge of what our chakras actually are and why it is important to learn how to create balance among them. We will explore the universal energies and how such energies can be found in everything. As well as energy, we will appreciate how vibrational frequencies play a role in our healing.

You might be able to learn enough about chakras from a blog or two, but then you may come back asking why there hasn't been the result you had expected, or that you feel like your emotions have moved to the other extreme rather than a balance.

This is why I always begin a book with plenty of detail and history so that you can get a complete feel for the concepts of chakras. Here, we will learn about the direction and strength of the energy that flows through us, and most importantly, we are going to look at the safe practices.

Before we work on techniques to awaken our chakras and find balance, we have to learn exactly what a blocked chakra feels like and identify exactly what it is we hope to gain.

CHAKRAS 101

The very first thing I wanted to do during my research phase was to meet someone who had benefited from unblocking their chakras. I didn't want to talk to a healer, or even have a chakra cleansing session. I wanted an honest conversation over a cup of coffee with an everyday person. This is when I met Helen.

Helen worked as an administrator in a hospital. She was grateful to have a job but there were a lot of negative things about it. She saw horrible cases, witnessed people suffering and had to cope with the tense emotions of patients and families on a daily basis. She was single and her family lived in another state. Her social life involved her pet dog. She was quiet, timid, sweet, and you could tell that she would never say no to doing something for others, even if it meant great sacrifices for herself.

She rarely cooked for herself and admitted to not having the best diet. She constantly had colds and sore throats and didn't have the energy or the inclination to exercise. She didn't want to meet new friends and go out because she didn't feel emotionally strong enough.

After meeting with a chakra expert, Helen told me how her life had changed. Most significantly, was her job. She felt more energetic at work. Each patient that came through the doors was no longer a problem for her. She saw herself as their solution. Her attitude had changed, and this allowed her to appreciate her role in their care. Being more emotionally aware, Helen became better at helping the patients and this resulted in the patients being nicer.

At the end of her day, she didn't feel so burdened by her awful day at work and felt she wanted to start doing things. Her experience with the chakra expert had been a positive one and so she joined a yoga class to continue learning more. Here, she met new people and she made plans with them. She met a lovely man and though she was still a little shy when talking about her feelings, the happiness radiated from her.

I knew at this point I had only spoken to one person. But I also knew that Helen had no reason to exaggerate her experience. It lit a spark. If Helen could unblock her chakras and notice such a difference, what other possibilities could be achieved?

So, how can our chakras be used to make the changes we want? Let's begin by looking at what chakras are exactly.

WHAT ARE CHAKRAS?

In the simplest terms, chakras are energy wheels that run the length of our spine. It is a very intricate subject as each chakra is linked to certain areas of the body. The chakras are related to a specific colour and have individual traits. All of these points are important to know in order to gain the most benefit.

Chakra- meaning wheel (pronounced /sha-kra/)

For a clearer mind and a healthier body, energy needs to flow through our bodies. When we experience an imbalance, it often means that one or all of our chakras are blocked, and this prevents energy from flowing. There are 7 principal chakras, the first at the base of our spine and the final one at the crown of our head.

Imagine each of your chakras as a water wheel. When the first water wheel spins correctly, it will pour water into the next, and allow this one to start spinning and so on. When someone throws a stick into the first water wheel, none of the others will receive any water. Our energy can be sat at the base of our spine, around the first chakra, but only when we remove the metaphorical stick, our energy will start to flow.

For now, we will just touch on the main functions of each chakra as each one has a dedicated chapter later on. In some spiritual teachings, you will see 12 or even 22 chakras. The core 7 chakras are related to the body, the additional ones are related to spirituality. Here, we will talk about 12 but for the rest of the book, the focus will be on the 7.

Root Chakra (associated colour-red)

This is this first chakra that is found at the base of your spine. It is connected to your tailbone, legs, feet, bladder and large intestine. The Root Chakra is related to power and when blocked, you may feel that you don't have the power you need to get yourself out of a situation.

Sacral Chakra (associated colour-orange)

As it is close to the reproductive organs, the Sacral Chakra is about sex and fertility. It can also impact your spleen, gallbladder, and kidneys. There is a strong relationship with honesty, and in particular, an honest sex life where you take responsibility for your sexual activities.

Solar Plexus Chakra (associated colour- yellow)

You can detect your Solar Plexus Chakra in your chest area. It points to your pride and confidence and if blocked, you may struggle to feel good about your achievements. If you have problems with your digestive system, small intestine, or pancreas, you might need some healing in this area.

Heart Chakra (associated colour- green)

Close to your heart, unblocking this chakra can have wonderful results on your relationships and the love you feel. However, when blocked, you may experience heartbreak or issues with your lungs, shoulders, arms, hands, and/or the thymus gland (the creator of cells which help our immune system).

Throat Chakra (associated colour- blue)

The Throat Chakra sits just over your vocal cords and is essential for communication. If blocked, you might feel like nobody seems to understand your point of view or that they just aren't listening. It can also impact your mouth, including the tongue and gums, your neck, glands, and even perspiration.

Third Eye Chakra (associated colour- indigo)

Sitting between your eyes just on the forehead, the Third Eye Chakra not only relates to good vision but the ability to foresee the circumstances in your life. The energy in this wheel can help improve your instincts and alleviate problems with your ears, nose, throat and brain.

Crown Chakra (associated colour- purple)

At the highest point of our physical body, the Crown Chakra is our closest connection with the divine. It is often linked to positive karma. For religious people, prayer can help to develop your divine connection, for the non-religious, we can practise meditation. It can affect our nervous system and the pituitary gland (the master gland that secretes hormones into our bloodstream).

Picturing my colourful chakras running up my spine always made me think of the multicoloured ice poles and my legs were the stick. The colours continue for the additional 5 chakras:

- 8th chakra- seafoam green, it activates our spiritual skills
- 9th chakra- blue-green, the skills we have learnt from our life experiences
- 10th Chakra- pearl white, awakening the divine creativity
- 11th chakra- pink-orange, advanced spiritual skills such as telekinesis
- 12th chakra- gold, the connection with the cosmos

As we are concerned with physical and emotional healing, it won't be necessary for us to talk about the 8th to 12th chakras, however, it is still a very interesting area if you want to learn more.

THE HISTORY OF CHAKRAS

Like so many things in the world, the west tends to take credit for things that have been around for years. In this case, when chakras reached the west around 100 years ago, we didn't claim to invent the idea of chakras, but look what we did to celebrations like Halloween and Christmas and you can see where I am coming from.

3,000 years ago, chakras were mentioned in the Upanishads, the religious texts of Hinduism. However, the English term of energy centres has also been found in Jewish, Egyptian, and Christian texts.

As with many of the ancient Hindu teachings found in the Upanishads, the knowledge and wisdom were not passed down through writing but orally. When the concepts reached the west, we began to create books about chakras.

Because of the age of the chakra teachings and the traditional methods of teaching, the main concept has remained the same, but many interpretations have developed along the way. This is most noticeable when talking about the number of chakras. Everyone agrees that there are 7 main chakras, but the additional energy wheels cause debate, with some even believing there are as many as 114.

Over time, the precise location of the chakras has also been debated. This is because they aren't organs or sets of tissues and bones. The Heart Chakra is associated with the heart, but it isn't over the heart. Some believe that it is in the centre of the chest while others feel it is to the left, above the heart.

Yoga was also first mentioned in the Upanishads and this practice has seen a great number of changes too. As yoga and chakra healing has matured to meet the ever-evolving needs of human-ity, we begin to see how the original teachings that already varied from region to region, have adapted to cultural influences.

HOW CULTURAL CHANGES HAVE INFLUENCED THE DIRECTION OF OUR ENERGETIC FLOW

It fascinates me how even those with higher spiritual awareness can still disagree on which way our energy flows. Does it pass up through our body, or does it flow down? Previously, we focused on the energy that flowed from our Root Chakra up to our Crown Chakra. This was because of the importance of attaining a higher state of consciousness and your energy needed to be driven upwards towards the divine. It was a case of mind over matter. The elevated levels of stress we suffer from today means that we should be trying to ground our energies. This helps us to remain connected with our physical self and enables us to calm down, even reduce the stress and anxiety we feel.

Who are we to argue with the great Hindu teachers? These teachers shared their wisdom and allowed their students to create their own process based on their experiences. I try to follow their example, particularly when deciding whether our energy flows up or down.

Visualisation of your energy is an essential part of chakra heal-ing. I try not to focus on whether my energy is flowing up or down, after all, I am a little greedy and I want to gain a better understanding of my higher consciousness and at the same time I want to reduce my stress. I like to visualise my energy spreading throughout my body, touching the areas that need it the most.

As you experiment with the techniques, you may find that in certain circumstances, you will benefit more from imagining your energy flowing up out of your body and towards the divine. I found this helped when I needed inspiration and to find creative ways to solve problems.

Other times I felt that parts of my body required a greater flow of energy, so I concentrated on opening the flow of energy and directing it to where it was most needed, whether that was up, down or all around. The more you practise, the more aware you will become of the directional flow of your energy and it is important that with regards to healing, we are all looking for different outcomes.

HOW DO CHAKRAS WORK?

Everything in the world has energy. It is something we tend not to think about as we don't have time to stop and look around. Every cell in our body releases energy. The kind of energy and how much depends on the functions of the cells. Up to now science and philosophy can agree.

Scientists, however, can't prove their existence because they aren't made of physical matter. So, this requires a leap of faith for those who prefer to follow the facts. I tend to compare chakras to love. You know what it feels like even if you can't see it or touch it.

Chakras can spin either clockwise or anticlockwise. When spinning clockwise, energy is pushed out of our body into a field around you.

Anticlockwise chakras draw energy from the world around you and pull it into your body. These powerful wheels of energy can be open or blocked. They can even be overactive or underactive.

The chakras use the endocrine system and the nervous system to interact with the physical and energetic body. Each one is located near and works with one of the endocrine glands or a plexus (a group of nerves). This is how working to unblock a particular chakra can help to heal certain parts of the body related to that endocrine gland or plexus.

We can use chakras to heal parts of our consciousness too. Your senses, perception of reality and the various states of awareness are divided into 7 groups and associated with a chakra. When a certain part of your consciousness is stressed or suffering, you will likely feel the tension on or around that chakra. This is why your legs might start to shake when you are nervous. The physical symptoms are a sign of our consciousness telling us of a problem within that chakra. Your legs will probably stop shaking once the nervous situation is over, but if a problem like a heartache, anxiety, or depression are not dealt with, the connected chakra will continue to present physical symptoms of the suffering.

If we go through a negative experience that produces low-frequency energy, the chakra that it is linked to may close as a form of protection. When we avoid handling our negative emotions the chakra can also close. This is how I was able to understand my problems. I knew that something was wrong, but I couldn't physically put my finger on the problem. It was the tension across my body that I felt like a form of immense pressure.

WHY ARE CHAKRA COLOURS IMPORTANT?

Another thing that surprised me was the significance of the colours. I had always known that red was the colour of wealth, green of peace and nature and so on. I assumed that the colour was relevant for this reason. In fact, the colour is important because of the vibrations it gives off. Go with me on this one!

The light that we see produces electromagnetic waves that vibrate through time and space. The frequency of vibrations allows us to see different colours. Red has low-frequency electromagnetic waves whereas purple is a high-frequency colour. The waves can be measured in nanometres and we can understand more about its energetic strength.

WHAT INFLUENCES THE BALANCE OF OUR CHAKRAS?

Our daily lives are full of experiences both good and bad that can impact the balance of our chakras. The hug of a loved one or the smile of your child stimulates our body and creates a small change electromagnetically. Watching the news causes us to feel sorrow and shame for those worse off than we are. Even stubbing your little toe can adjust the energy we have within us. Each action is registered in one of the seven chakras, depending on the physical part of the body or the emotions we feel.

Different cultural environments can play a role in the balance of our chakras. For example, in western cultures, we place emphasis on mental abilities and scientific theories. This leads to the third chakra dominating over the others. Mediterranean countries can experience a stronger 2nd Chakra because of the sensual and expressive culture.

Our body tries to maintain a balance within the chakras but with so much going on, it is a challenging mission. When one chakra is underactive, another one will work overtime. This draws energy away from other parts of your body. Despite trying to fix the wrong, we tend to feel more imbalance.

Our lifestyle will also determine the flow of our energy and potential imbalance. A balanced diet is essential in order to feed each chakra with the right type of fuel. Again, we will talk more of this when we go into the details of each chakra. There is a massive difference between working at a desk all day and being able to get out and experience the smells and colours of the natural world.

Knowing exactly what chakras are and how they function is the first step to exploring the relationship between our energy centres and how we can look to unblock them. There is no end of unit tests and I know that you might not remember all of the names and exact characteristics just yet, that's ok. For now, it is great that you are aware of the seven chakras running along your spine and you are ready to learn how to unblock them.

POWERFUL HEALING CENTRES

As we work together through this chapter, I will provide examples of potential signs and symptoms so that you can relate to the concepts more easily. Be careful though, our brain has a way of tricking us into thinking that this is the exact same problem that you have. Going through the different understandings, take a moment to see how this relates to you and your chakras. Hopefully, by the end of this chapter, you will have a list of the chakras that you feel are blocked or overactive.

HOW DO BLOCKED CHAKRAS AFFECT YOUR HEALTH?

Each of our chakras will contain an element of Prana, the ultimate pure healing energy. When chakras are blocked you might notice a range of symptoms because it's this healing energy which keeps us happy and healthy.

Though we have touched on how each chakra can impact the body, let's take a closer look at what you could experience when the chakras are blocked.

Root Chakra

The Root Chakra is like the foundations of your body and will provide you with support. It is closely related to our survival instincts, the need for food, shelter, and security. Because of the stress we feel when our basic needs are not met, a blocked Root Chakra can lead to anxiety disorders and our fears taking control of our lives. With excessive nervousness, we may experience problems with our bladders, like when you go to the toilet 5 times before an exam. There could also be issues with the lower back and limbs.

Sacral Chakra

When this chakra is blocked, you may have a problem expressing your sexual pleasure as well as that sense of completeness when we are happy. It can also point to how you express your creativity. When blocked, you may have ideas but be unable to find the right way to go about turning them into a reality. In terms of physical health, you might have problems with your reproductive system, sexual dysfunctions or a lack of sexual appetite.

Solar Plexus Chakra

We rely on the Solar Plexus Chakra for our determination and commitment. It is the control we have over ourselves and the unique power that we possess. A lack of confidence may be noticed when this chakra is blocked. You might also find it more difficult to make the right decision and spend a lot of time procrastinating. These negative emotions you feel about yourself can lead to bursts of anger. Due to the location, it is most often associated with digestive problems.

Heart Chakra

As well as the logical connection to the heart and how we give and receive love, the Heart Chakra being blocked can make it more difficult to forgive and we feel less compassionate. A blocked Heart Chakra can bring about some very powerful negative emotions including jealousy, hatred, and grief. You might find it impossible to forgive others and move on. If you are not in a relationship, a blocked Heart Chakra can make it far more difficult to find love. Physically, you might have a low immune system, heart or lung problem, high or low blood pressure or poor circulation.

Throat Chakra

This chakra is the ruler of your communication. You might think you have expressed yourself well, but others don't seem to follow what you are saying. You might struggle to find the words for the right situation. I realised I might have a problem with a blocked Throat Chakra when I met with the vicar to plan my grandad's funeral. The first thing I said when I opened the door was "Good God you're tall", followed by "Jesus sorry", and I just couldn't shut up. When blocked, you may also find it difficult to listen, which is equally important in successful communication. There might be thyroid issues and tension across your shoulders up to your neck through to your head.

Third Eye Chakra

As well as your intuition, many believe that the Third Eye Chakra is the link between your physical self and the world around you. It is critical to unblock this chakra if you want to be able to clear the cloudiness around situations and see things for how they really are. I found this necessary when planning practical goals that I knew I had the skills to obtain. A judgemental attitude, depression, and/or anxiety may be accompanied by headaches, dizzy spells, and other potential health issues related to the brain such as your memory.

Crown Chakra

When open and balanced, you can benefit from being fully aware of who you are in relation to the rest of the universe. For some, this is about gaining a spiritual connection but for others, it is about feeling your normal self, well and positive. When it is blocked, you can feel as if you don't know what your purpose is, or that you are not connected to anything. Without connections, you can feel as if you are very much alone in the world and this can be extremely distressing. A blocked Crown Chakra can be associated with neurological disorders, nerve pain, recurring migraines, insomnia, and depression.

WHAT MIGHT YOU EXPERIENCE IF YOUR CHAKRAS ARE OVERACTIVE

The above physical and emotional symptoms are what you can expect to feel when one or more of the chakras are blocked. When they are underactive, it is quite possible that you will experience milder symptoms. So, if you are experiencing headaches, it could be that your Crown Chakra is underactive rather than blocked, which could lead to migraines.

When your chakras are overactive, you might experience some of the following emotions:

Root Chakra- you might be nervous, especially when it comes to change. You may also be overly obsessed with material objects, possibly greedy.

Sacral Chakra- it is possible that you are too quick to form relationships. You might be too sensitive causing you to be moody. You might like the drama in life and have a habit of crossing boundaries.

Solar Plexus Chakra- you may feel the need to dominate others and you can come across as aggressive. You might expect perfection from yourself and others.

Heart Chakra- your love could be too much for some and you appear to be clingy in relationships. You may not have enough boundaries and tend to say yes just to please others.

Throat Chakra- it is likely that you talk too much and you fail to listen to others. This could be to the extent that you are verbally abusive and criticise others.

Third Eye Chakra- you may struggle to concentrate, often slipping into daydreams or even hallucinations. As you aren't in touch with reality, it might be hard for you to use your good judgement.

Crown Chakra- your focus on spirituality may lead you to abandon your bodily needs. It might be hard for you to control your feelings.

WHAT TO EXPECT WHEN YOU TAKE THE TIME TO AWAKEN, BALANCE, AND GRADUALLY OPEN YOUR CHAKRAS

When the chakras are all functioning in the right way, the flow of energy within your body will be corrected and you will gain an overall sense of balance in yourself and your life.

This will be achieved when you become aware of certain properties of chakras, including:

- The different qualities of energies within a chakra and their frequencies
- The correct level of intensity, so not overactive or underactive
- Whether they should be flowing clockwise or anticlockwise
- The polarity, meaning whether the energy flows inward or outward.

The experiences we have been through in life will not only affect one chakra. The 7 chakras are interlinked. While we will focus our healing efforts on one or maybe two chakras, there will be a positive impact on all of them.

Most significantly, you will notice a balance between your spiritual side and your physical self. The lower chakras include the Root Chakra, the Sacral Chakra, and the Solar Plexus Chakra. These lower chakras generally reflect your physical self, how you view yourself and the emotions you feel. They flow up to the Heart Chakra. The higher chakras, the Throat Chakra, Third Eye Chakra and the Crown Chakra, are generally concentrated on your spirituality and higher consciousness. These connect to the lower energy wheels via the Heart Chakra.

We will strive to gain a balance between your physical and spiritual self. This will allow you to experience a better body, whether you want to strengthen a certain part of you or overcome an illness. With this, you can view yourself in a positive light and see an improvement in the feelings you have for yourself. But we will also work on the spiritual side to make sure you feel complete. This doesn't imply that you will all of a sudden discover your religious beliefs, it is about being more conscious of who you truly are.

HOW WILL YOU KNOW IF YOUR CHAKRAS ARE BALANCED

Similarly to the precise location of the chakras, it is difficult to put a finger on what it is like when the lower and higher chakras are all balanced. It's that moment when you realise that life is good or when you wake up one morning and you suddenly appreciate that you don't have the weight of the world on your shoulders. You are happy and you genuinely feel great and optimistic. It's hard to imagine because, for many of us, we have put up with years of just trying to survive, we can't remember what this feeling is actually like.

For me, it was the sensation of the sea covering your feet. The contrast of the warm sand below and the cool water above. You know the feeling of working hard on a hot summer's day, completing your entire to-do list and sitting down with a cold beer to take in your success. Or waking up on a Sunday with the whole day just for you. It's freedom from the life you wanted to leave behind you.

You will sense the balance of your chakras when you are aware of how each of the seven energy wheels is functioning. You will see great changes in so many areas of your life as if the puzzle pieces are finally fitting together.

Why We Don't Want to Open Our Chakras

Our goal in this book is to balance our chakras. Just as one problem in your life can affect a number of other areas, one imbalanced chakra can cause the others to become out of balance, interrupting the complete flow of the energy in your body.

When your chakras are balanced, you will notice that it is easier to heal, both physically and mentally. You will have a greater sense of who you are and what you and your body need. You are more aware of the world around you and you can learn how to use what the world offers you to your advantage. Because of heightened awareness of your own emotions and those of others, you will be better at communicating and creating more meaningful relationships.

With that in mind, I wanted to quickly mention the reason why we want to balance our chakras and not open them. Opening chakras before you are ready can be dangerous as you aren't prepared for the amount of openness you can receive. Your true nature can become more powerful, this initially seems like a good thing, but you must learn how to cope with negativity and pain. If not, you may end up adjusting to this negativity and even projecting it onto others around you.

If we haven't had enough time to learn about our chakras, opening them could lead to a rush of emotions that we cannot protect ourselves from, even feelings that aren't our own and that could be coming from those around us. If you take on the negative emotions of others you will be overwhelmed, and this could lead to anxiety and depression. Ironically, you could find yourself in a worse situation than you are currently in.

Before jumping into opening chakras, it is critical that you learn how to cleanse and slowly awaken them so that you can better control your emotions and the potential outcomes. You do not want to open your chakras and find yourself in a realm that you can't handle.

I have witnessed first-hand what happens when people try to force open their chakras. They feel like they are in a desperate situation and this requires drastic actions. Highly sensitive people have rushed the process instead of taking the time to awaken and then balance chakras. I have seen the strength of other people's negativity consuming them and causing them to do all sorts of extreme things. In some cases, it was incredibly hard to come back from.

The point is not to scare you, but just to say that there is a logical, safe process to working with chakras and learning how to balance them. This is the process that we will work on throughout the book.

WHICH TO TACKLE FIRST; BALANCING CHAKRAS OR HEALING EMOTIONS?

So, here is the chicken and egg conundrum of chakras and our emotions- which do we tackle first? By the time your body sends the right signals to let you know you are thirsty, you are already dehydrated, the same goes for chakras. By the time your body tells you that there is an imbalance in your chakras, the emotional damage has already been caused. Do you start by working to understand and overcome your emotions so that you can balance your chakras, or do you focus on balancing your chakras to help your emotions?

Changing one thing can often negatively impact something else, albeit briefly. If you have ever had a massage you might feel sensational straight after, but the massage has caused a release of chemicals in our body and this can cause us to feel achy or groggy the following day.

For this reason, we might have to use other methods alongside the balancing of chakras in order to successfully release one symptom without allowing the consequences to take their toll. I am a huge fan of yoga and meditation. Both have been used in

Hinduism and other religions together with chakra healing. Mantras are another tool which enabled me to really see some amazing changes in my life. Let's take a look at how you too can benefit from some of the other life-changing techniques from the Eastern teachings.

PART II
UNDERSTANDING THE TECHNIQUES USED TO BALANCE CHAKRAS

It's pretty fascinating stuff when you dig a little deeper than the top layer. For me, it was almost like just understanding that these spinning wheels existed enabled me to become more aware of my flow of energy and the impact of this slightest thing that can, in turn, have an impact on other chakras.

Part 2 is all about how we can begin to create a balance. We will cover a wide range of techniques that aren't only associated with Hinduism. If you have ever wanted to explore the healing benefits of Reiki and reflexology, it's time to get comfortable and read on.

If you never understood why a certain smell calms you down in an instant, we will talk about some of the key essential oils that are used in Aromatherapy. A book about balancing the chakras just wouldn't be complete without exploring yoga and meditation. And you will be able to discover ways of combining various techniques to find the best healing methods for you.

I will warn you now, part 2 touches on some of the ideas, let's call it the appetisers before the main course which is coming up in part 3!

MANTRAS AND MEDITATION, THE KEYS TO THE HEALING KINGDOM

I had already dabbled in a little yoga, but I was far from an expert in my early days. It is not essential that you have practised yoga to enjoy the benefits of meditation, nor vice versa. At the same time, you don't need to be able to speak Sanskrit or believe in the deities to appreciate the effects of mantras.

This chapter is going to explain the difference between affirmations and mantras and how both of these tools can be used to further create balance in our lives. Then we will move onto meditation, an area that I personally found extremely challenging, but I am so glad I was determined enough to stick at it.

WHAT IS A MANTRA?

Mantras are words or sentences that focus on sounds rather than the actual meaning. Most traditional mantras were originally prayers or songs that were used to speak to the gods and gain a higher conscious connection to the spiritual world. Like chakras, mantras were first mentioned in the Upanishads and are a key part of the Hindu teachings that have been passed down orally over thousands of years.

Whether meditating or just chanting mantras, the repetition of the sounds is a tool which allows your mind to focus, to stop working overtime regarding our chaotic lives and to simply be in the moment. Each sound in the mantra has a specific vibration that can encourage immense healing in the body.

Mantras are usually repeated 108 times and people will often hold a mala to help them keep track of the number of repetitions. A mala is a set of 108 beads which you slide your finger over each one as you say your mantra. This is another tool that will help you to remain focused on your healing rather than the number of times you have said your mantra.

When chanting, or even repeating a mantra silently, certain parts of the brain are activated so that we feel less stress and more relaxed. The positive vibrations help to reduce the negativity we feel.

Western science has even taken an interest in the healing benefits of mantras. To date, a number of scientific studies have been carried out and all with very similar outcomes. Scientists have found that the regular chanting of mantras helps oxygenate the brain, lower the heart rate and blood pressure and calm brainwave activity. It can also increase focus and assist in curing many ailments.

To gain the most from mantras, it is recommended to chant them for 10-15 minutes in the morning and evening. More specifically, many of the mantras should be chanted before or during sunrise, however, I found that starting my day with my mantras was a great way to begin with a positive outlook. Last thing at night is a good time to calm the mind before falling asleep.

There are probably hundreds of thousands of mantras, all with various purposes and intentions. If you want to learn more about mantras, you can find my book Healing Mantras. It takes a closer look at the history of mantras and how they have a positive impact on healing. There are hundreds of examples and even pronunciation tips. The group that we are going to look at are bija mantras.

WHAT IS A BIJA MANTRA?

Everything we say produces sound waves which create certain vibrational frequencies. Bija mantras are also known as seed mantras, these one-syllable seed sounds have no literal translation but the vibrations they create can lead to incredible physical and emotional healing.

More specifically, bija mantras were created with the intention to create a balance between the body and mind and even the soul. This is done by tapping into the unique rhythms and pulses the different parts of our body have.

The healing benefits of sound waves have gained more credibility in the last half a century or so due to the study of Psychoacoustics. Our cells are made up of 70% water, sound waves travel through water five times faster than they do through air. So, what one would call sound energy for healing, others would today call sound therapy.

I'm still fascinated by how such small words, even sounds could stimulate all of my senses and allow me to become more aware of everything around me. The bija mantras for chakras really help us to concentrate on your body and what it needs at the time.

BIJA MANTRAS FOR CHAKRAS

There is one bija mantra for each chakra. It is most beneficial if you are sitting down in a cross-legged position if you are comfortable. Grab a cushion or a yoga mat if it helps. It is important that you are sat up straight and if possible, in a calm environment.

- Root Chakra- Lam
- Sacral Chakra- Vam
- Solar Plexus Chakra- Ram
- Heart Chakra- Yam
- Throat Chakra- Ham
- Third Eye Chakra- U or Aum
- Crown Chakra- Om or Aum

In each of these seeds or syllables, the a is pronounced as u, so you produce a more throaty, deeper sound. Lam is pronounced lum, the same sound as plum. The exception is the Third Eye Chakra which is pronounced like the U in uber.

Chanting one of the bija mantras to awaken your chakra requires a focus on the area you are aiming to heal and create balance in. Let's look at some examples of how to use these mantras.

Sandra had pulled a muscle in her calf and needed to allow for more energy in her Sacral Chakra. She repeated "Vam" 432 times. This was 4 sets of 108. She did this in the morning and evening but also before she went for her daily walk.

Charlie had recently separated from his wife. He felt a tightness in his chest and was in complete despair. He chanted "Yam" 108 times in four sessions throughout the day.

Carol felt that she was slightly overweight. She also suffered from frequent headaches and had problems sleeping. In this case, we needed to work on two of her chakras; the Root Chakra and the Third Eye Chakra. In order to concentrate fully on the area that needs healing, you should complete one set of the bija mantra and then a second set for a different chakra. Carol chanted "Lam" 108 times followed by "U" 108 times. She did this twice a day but when she began to feel a headache coming on, she also stopped what she was doing and repeated "U", the Third Eye Chakra 108 times.

It is also recommended that all mantras are repeated for a minimum period of 30 days. For the maximum benefits, you should also focus on the colour that is associated with the particular chakra you are working on. This will help create the correct vibration frequency.

Finally, don't forget your breathing. It must be slow, deep, and controlled. Maintaining a steady rhythm with your breathing will help you not to rush through the process. Visualisation and breathing are so important when using bija mantras for chakra healing, we will touch on both in more detail towards the end of this chapter.

What Are Affirmations?

The mind is both incredibly powerful and incredibly busy! It is estimated that we have between 45,000 and 51,000 thoughts per day. Even imagining that we have between 150 and 300 thoughts per minute is exhausting. Then to think that for a large percentage of people, 80% of these thoughts are negative.

"There is nothing either good or bad but thinking makes it so."

— *WILLIAM SHAKESPEARE*

This quote from Shakespeare makes a lot of sense. Realistically, we all have to do the grocery shopping. This is neither good nor bad until we relate an emotion to it. The supermarket is going to be packed and on top of that, I literally need everything-shopping becomes a negative thought. If I buy those ingredients, I can try that new recipe I have been meaning to make-shopping becomes a positive thought.

The problem is that today's society is a rather negative one. There is not a great deal of positive news on TV or in the papers. It's easier to complain about life than it is to see the positive. But this is incredibly draining on our mind and it's not necessary. The trick is learning how to start thinking more positively. This is where affirmations can help us.

An affirmation is a short sentence that is simple and has great power to the user. Repeating an affirmation changes the way we think and behave and when repeated enough times with the right conviction, will allow a person to become more positive. When choosing the appropriate affirmation for you can make the necessary changes even by just thinking about it.

Affirmations are used to create motivation, which can help you achieve the goals you have set. You may also find it easier to reach your goals because by positively altering your subconscious, it becomes easier to meet new people. They can enable you to activate your inner energies and help you bring about the changes that you want to make.

HOW TO USE AFFIRMATIONS TO CREATE A MORE POSITIVE YOU

In the first place, you need to make sure your affirmation is relevant to you and has meaning. It must fit with your intentions. Here are some excellent affirmations that I have used for myself as well as people I have helped:

- I am fearless
- I can do this
- I choose what I become
- I wink at a challenge
- I am successful
- I am healthy
- I am happy
- My life is full of fun
- I believe in myself
- Life is good

If you choose the affirmation "I can do this", you need to know exactly what it is you want to achieve and as you repeat the words, create an image in your mind of what it is you can do. If you want to improve your health, you have to visualise yourself as a healthy person as you say the words.

As with the bija mantras, you should repeat your affirmation at least twice first thing in the morning and last thing at night. I always use mine throughout the day when I need to believe in myself a little more. Again, commit to at least 30 days of using your affirmations. Did you know that before astronauts are permitted to join a space mission, they must practise all of their new skills for at least 30 days? It is generally believed that 30 days is how long it takes for something to 'stick'.

It is possible that you need an affirmation that is more specific to you and in this case, you can create your own. When you do, there are a few things that you should remember.

1. Your affirmation must ring true to you, something that you feel is relevant for the situation you face. Keep it short and simple.
2. Your affirmation must be positive. In order to create positivity, your words need to be positive.
3. Your affirmation must be in the present tense. Your subconscious is only concerned with the present, not the past or the future. You need to tell your subconscious how you want to be now.

I have always found it helpful to keep a note of the changes I feel over the 30 days. This will help you to be aware of your emotions and when your affirmation is making an impact. It is highly likely that if you are determined and consistent, you see positive changes sooner.

VISUALISATION, BREATHING, AND MEDITATION

Ok, so breathing is probably not the challenging aspect here, although not everyone has the ability to completely focus on their breathing without their minds wandering off. Visualisation and meditation require great concentration and focus, and this certainly doesn't come easily to everyone. Let's tackle them separately.

VISUALISATION

Visualisation involves using your imagination to focus on behaviours or situations that you wish to happen in your life. This could be getting a promotion, finding love, or overcoming certain illnesses or physical problems, etc. Visualisation is not just about seeing yourself in this position, but engaging all of your senses, imagining the smells and sounds of what you want to achieve.

This doesn't mean that if you imagine yourself how you want to be, the next day it will simply occur. The mind and the body are linked but it takes repeated visualisation for the mind to communicate the changes to the body and for the body to start making these subtle changes. It's a working progress.

I will admit that the concept was difficult for me to get my head around in the beginning. Surely if it were that simple, we would all be doing it and we would all be happier. I needed something a little more solid before I tried visualisation because, in order for it to work, you have to truly believe it will.

Depending on who you talk to, visualisation will have different names. Some people call it guided imagery or mental imagery. In the world of sports, it is often called sports visualisation.

Many athletes will use sports visualisation to see themselves winning their race or game. One person that caught my attention was Michael Phelps. Most famous for being the most decorated Olympian of all time, few people know that he suffers from Marfan Syndrome, which can affect the bones, muscles, ligaments, and the aorta. Phelps created a mental videotape of each step of his race, from the starting block to winning the race. He repeated his "tape" before going to bed and when he woke up. He also used the technique during training sessions.

I was starting to believe.

Then I came across a study related to chronic pain and fibromyalgia. Chronic pain is defined as an ongoing pain that lasts for at least three months. Shockingly, around 10 to 40% of the population suffer from chronic pain which has a massive knock-on effect on the economy. People who suffer from fibromyalgia experience chronic pain and fatigue.

Those that took part in the 2014 study reported that after practising visualisation daily for 6 weeks experienced a reduction of chronic pain deriving from the muscles, skeleton, or from fibromyalgia.

There were plenty more studies I found about the positive effects on the immune system as well as stress and anxiety and this is when I felt more convinced that I could also benefit.

HOW TO USE VISUALISATION FOR HEALING

It all begins with finding a comfortable position and relaxing your breathing. Start by focusing on the muscles in your feet and making sure they are completely relaxed, then work your way up through your body until every muscle is relaxed. You can go from head to toe if you prefer.

Start to imagine what it is you want to achieve. If you have a cold that you want to get rid of, you might imagine your body fighting the virus. If you want to quit smoking you could imagine your lungs breathing in the clean, fresh air. Then start to concentrate on stimulating your senses. What exactly does that clean air smell like, fresh-cut grass, pine? What can you hear, the birds, the wind in the leaves? Can you feel that breeze on your face? Once you have created the complete image in your mind, repeat it. Every time you practise your visualisation, replay the image you created.

Sometimes, people need a little help, especially when you first begin. You might want to consider joining a group or asking for someone to help you talk you through your image until you feel you can do it alone. You could also look for some online visualisation tools.

When we use the visualisation technique to awaken our chakras, we completely focus on the chakra that we want to heal. Begin again with breathing and relaxing all of your muscles, then start to imagine the wheel spinning and the energy beginning to flow, sense the power of this energy and the positive impact you want it to make on your body. Imagine the colour of the chakra.

Have you ever seen a fiery eye in a firework display? When I use visualisation for healing chakras, I like to imagine the chakra as the fiery eye. It's the firework that is often bright, intense lights that spin around. Picturing this, for me, was the perfect way to imagine the chakra full of positive healing energy.

BREATHING AND MEDITATION

Meditation was another slight struggle for me but for a different reason. I felt that the visualisation required a belief that it would work. Meditation for me required emptying of the mind and this is what I found hard. Even though I was determined, things kept pushing into my brain and distracting me, tasks that needed to be done, feelings, the shopping list. In the beginning, I had to keep restarting over and over and I almost felt frustrated. I wanted to experience the benefits of meditation and gain some inner peace and clarity.

At this point, I learnt why breathing is so important. By concentrating on your breathing, your brain is kept busy and it helps to prevent it from being distracted by other thoughts. But when you think about it, breathing is quite boring and how much can you really think about this involuntary action. Surprisingly, quite a lot. Before you begin meditating, consider these things about a simple breath:

- Your breath is probably the simplest yet most powerful thing you have. All it does is go in and go out, it can't change direction and we can't speed it up to get it out of the way and do something more interesting. On the other hand, without it, you cannot survive.

- Concentrating on your breathing allows you to focus on something that occurs in your body rather than your mind. Most of us are so overwhelmed by our own thinking that we don't concentrate on our body. When you imagine your breath passing through your body and the oxygen moving through every inch of it, you begin to create a closer connection between the body and the mind, and you can enjoy the moment.

- Each breath is different. We can change the depth, and the duration, we can speed it up and slow it down at will. The curious thing about breathing is that it is something that we have complete control over, yet it is one of the few things that nobody tells us how to do it.
- Breathing allows our body a chance to regain balance after a fight or flight situation. Today, fight or flight can be anything from the stress of work to traffic or the kids fighting. When man came face to face with a predator, his breath would speed up and there would be tension in all of his muscles. After, man would have time to relax and find balance. We often don't give ourselves a chance to breathe after the stress we deal with. Mindfulness breathing or concentrating on your breathing is a chance for your body to relax and find balance again.

"When you own your breath, nobody can steal your peace."

— *AUTHOR UNKNOWN*

Once you begin to really think about the process of breathing, its significance and the fact that if you are breathing, you have something to celebrate, you will find that there is actually quite a lot to consider. This will really help you when you begin using mindful breathing to help with healing.

5 WAYS TO USE MINDFUL BREATHING FOR HEALING

1. Enlightenment

Meditating while mindful breathing opens your mind to deep insights that you may otherwise miss. It can awaken your mind and who you really are, and with enough practice, some are able to achieve enlightenment.

2. Relaxation

Breathing and meditation bring about a tranquillity that is rare in our everyday lives. It can help you to clear your mind so you can really relax. Even focusing on breathing in and out for a few minutes can help you to relax during moments of stress throughout the day.

3. Freeing yourself from negative thoughts

We have already seen just how much negativity passes through our mind in a single hour. It is useless trying to block out this negativity as it will just come back at another time. Instead, mindful breathing can enable you to identify the negativity and let it flow out with every breath, stopping it from becoming attached to you.

4. Inner Peace

Finding inner peace lets you free yourself from the stress and anxiety that are constantly present. It gives our mind and body a chance to experience calm. It's a moment of happiness which provides us with more power to face our problems later.

5. Understanding More About Your Body

When I was pregnant, I was intrigued by the idea of a contraction being the muscles in your body that are calling out for more oxygen and that is why breathing is so essential to help with pain management. Learning how your body reacts to your breathing can provide important information about who you are within your body and what your body needs.

The goal of meditation may be different for some but the principal reason for practising meditation and mindful breathing is to create a stronger connection between your mind and your body, to find peace, and balance, to be able to relax and deal with your negative thoughts so that you can enjoy a happier life. Achieving a higher awareness of yourself through meditation is easier when you learn how to focus on your breathing. This pulls you into the here and now and is a great way to appreciate that life is probably better than we tend to think.

Mantras, affirmations, visualisation, and meditation are simply phenomenal tools and when used the right way, can bring about the changes you need to start enjoying life more. These can be physical or emotional or a combination of both. These ancient

Eastern techniques are unique to the individual and you should allow time to experiment with them and learn exactly how they can be used with the specific chakras that you want to awaken.

Another practical tool that can help create a balance within our chakras is Chakra Astrology. The next stage of our journey will concern the connection between chakras and the planets.

CHAKRA ASTROLOGY

When we start talking about Astrology and the planets, my mind rushes straight back to geography classes in school. I remember the teacher repeating the mnemonic "My Very Educated Mother Just Served Nine Pizzas" because Pluto was still considered a planet then. As a child, you start to wonder why you need to remember such information.

I now wonder if the point of learning about the planets and the solar system was to simply remind us that we are part of something much larger and that universal balance is equally important as our internal balance. I also think that as we become adults, we become so wrapped up in the craziness of our own lives that we are unable to see the bigger picture.

The planets have an important role in who we are. I think it was probably in the 90s that astrology started to be the latest fashion. Can you remember Mystic Meg? Rushing out to buy the latest edition of Cosmopolitan to read your stars? What we did to the concept of astrology might have put some people off, but I promise, when you take away all the glitter and jazz, there is a great sense to how the planets affect our body and who we are.

The first breath we take after we are born is etched into our cells. A birth chart is an astrological tool that tells a person more about the planets at the time we took our first breath. Our birth chart describes our spiritual, physical and mental aspects.

Understanding the position and different aspects of the planets at the time of our birth can help us to appreciate the part we play in the universe and how we can ensure there is balance within ourselves.

We have already learnt of the immense amount of energy and power our chakras can have. Now consider the energy and power of the entire solar system. Each of our chakras is associated with a planet and tend to mimic the nature and characteristics of that planet. You might say that each of us is our own mini solar system within the solar system we studied at school.

Loka- meaning Planet

Loka also means the degree of level, and it is the level of our vital energies that are connected to the planets. Being in tune with the planets is another form of meditation that can help us to balance our chakras. Let's look at each of the chakras again but now in relation to the planets.

THE CONNECTION BETWEEN OUR CHAKRAS AND THE PLANETS

Before mankind started following the norms, we were great explorers. Our attention was first on our inner selves and then we turned to see how this related to the universe. From here, all of the wonderful spiritual traditions such as astrology and healing.

In ancient times, humans would observe the Planets and with time, they began to see a link between the location of the planets and experiences with the seven chakras. When the heavenly bodies moved, the effects were seen on things like our creativity, activity, and even the conflicts we have. This is how we began to appreciate the particular influences planets, the Sun and the Moon had on everything in the universe.

The Root Chakra: Mars

This chakra is related to the expression "I am" and has close ties to our ability to survive and the need for stability. When we are fully aware of our reality, we are able to leave our past behind us and live in the moment. This provides us with motivation. When the energies of Mars are agitated, we can notice feelings of guilt, fear, insecurity and even anger.

The Sacral Chakra: Venus

The expression "I feel" is related to our sensuality and tenderness. As Venus is the plant of worldly pleasures when all is balanced and well with Venus, we can enjoy the pleasures of the world. More specifically, we can do this with spontaneity and without becoming attached to these pleasures. We are comfortable with who we are in all senses, physically, emotionally, and sexually.

The Solar Plexus Chakra: The Sun

We all know how much better we feel when the sun is present, and the expression "I do" is seen in the increased determination to get things done on those bright days. We are more optimistic and confident about life. The Sun allows us to feel recharged and to take advantage of the skills and talents we have to achieve things. When all is right, our ego doesn't get in the way.

The Heart Chakra: The Moon

The Moon signifies the mother in Astrology and the two words are "I love". The Moon gives us support and nourishment, it can aid us with our boundaries. When everything flows correctly, there is a genuine sense of peace and joy. You are able to love and embrace love completely.

* * *

The Throat Chakra: Mercury

As the throat is tied to our speech, the expression is "I speak". If Mercury is in balance and functioning, we will find it easier to express ourselves, not only with our words but also with our creativity.

The Third Eye Chakra: Saturn

"I see" when Saturn enables us to think with great clarity you will have the insights to comprehend the consequences of your actions. If Saturn is good, the laws of karma, time, and life are understood.

The Crown Chakra: Jupiter

When Jupiter is well, we are able to receive wisdom on all levels. The expression "I understand" allows us to expand and to be generous. The power that Jupiter can give us when well-placed is the ability to understand the practicalities of life, people, as well as higher concepts

So now we know what the impact of various planets, the Sun and the Moon can have on our chakras, but we still haven't answered the question of how. For this, you will need some creative imagination!

Imagine yourself sitting crossed-legged and the chakras running in a vertical line from the base of the spine to the crown of your head. Now picture a circle around your body. From the top of the circle, there will be segments, 6 to the left and 6 to the right.

The outer segments are projected at a 30-degree angle and this represents the Root Chakra. Each segment from here is split into 30 degrees and represents the next chakra, each having a segment to the left and the right.

When a planet is in a projection area of one of the chakras, it will impact that chakra depending on the nature and characteristics of it. Notice that there is no segment dedicated to the Crown Chakra. This is because the Crown Chakra relates to the higher connection to the spiritual world and connects us to the divine.

The influence is also dependent on whether the planet is in the section of the chakra to the left or the right. The segments that are on the left of the circle will play a role in the receptive part, or the energy that is received. On the contrary, those that are to the right are influenced by the emissive side or the energy that is controlled.

Now let's look at the different chakras again with a focus on the receptive (left) and emissive (right) side when the planet is in line with the projected segment of the related chakra.

The Root Chakra

The receptive side points to material energy and physical action. There is plenty of activity on this level. It also shows that you have courageous friends in your corner.

When Mars falls to the emissive side, you will notice greater stability. The energy you feel will be more controlled yet there will still be plenty of action and more so, the courage may be coming from you.

The Sacral Chakra

Still related to sexual energy, on the receptive side, it indicates our sexual potential. Still, there is more to it than merely sex. The alignment allows you to meet people and be able to support them on a psychological level. It will enable you to find a passion for your interests and hobbies.

When Venus is in line with the emissive side of the Sacral Chakra, you will feel more seductive and appreciate the power of seduction. You might even find that you will be able to use these feelings to take back more control of your sexual power.

The Solar Plexus Chakra

You will feel more confident when the Sun is in the receptive side of your Solar Plexus Chakra. This is probably helped by the high-quality energy that you naturally feel and that radiates from those around you.

When the Sun is in your emissive side you will feel like you have more charisma. More significantly, you will have more willpower and determination and greater control over these emotions.

. . .

The Heart Chakra

To the left, you will receive love and the things you enjoy in life and be more respective. You will find it easy to soak up the energies around you and take information in from others or from the natural world.

Love will beam from you when the Moon appears on your right side, your feelings will be profound, and you will gain an inner perspective that is clearer when regarding the energies of this level.

The Throat Chakra

The receptive side relates to our passive intuition and you will be more receptive. You will see that it is easy to find your energy and you absorb it, soak it all in. You will also notice that you are intrigued by any information that others tell you, both spoken and written.

On the emissive side, your intuition is active, with a greater connection to other worlds. You have become a master of your understanding and mental control.

The Third Eye Chakra

On the one hand, your mental interests will be heightened, and you may feel the need to analyse things more. The memory will be better too. On the other hand, Saturn on the receptive side might point to a lack of resources and energy.

When Saturn falls to the emissive side, there will be mental creativity but there will also be a practical side to this. You find benefits to high levels of control and planning, and this could be truer with regards to your finances.

MEDITATION AND CHAKRA ASTROLOGY

You have probably picked up on my love for spiritualism by now, but I have so much respect for it because of the variety of ways that one can learn more about themselves and unlock their potential so that they can lead a more fulfilling life. One of these techniques is meditation. Meditation can have numerous forms from walking to even the mundane jobs we have like doing the laundry. It's all about your state of mind.

When we start to reveal the concepts of astrology and chakras it opens the door to appreciating that though we are here and living our own life, we are also a kind of observer, watching how the world changes around us. I feel like I am a weathervane placed in a field. While I remain still, I can see, experience and appreciate the changing weather. Standing in the peacefulness of the field, I am able to meditate on these changes and the effects on my life. I can witness all extremes from the storms to the sun.

HOW TO USE ASTROLOGY AND MEDITATION TO BENEFIT YOUR CHAKRAS

We begin by visualising the chakra that you wish to create more balance and focus on its location in the body. Concentrate on the energy and that each planet (or the Sun/Moon) is related to, focus on your breathing and imagine your body beginning filled with this energy. Remember that each heavenly body will also emit vibrations and a concentration on the certain vibrations can also encourage healing.

Rather than look at each chakra again, let's round this chapter up with a look at what you should concentrate on when visualising each of the heavenly bodies during meditation.

The Sun- imagine your conscious identity, how you are when you feel most alive. Meditate on your creativity and your attitude towards yourself. Imagine the pure energy and light from the sun filling your body and flowing towards the chakra you are visualising.

The Moon- when you focus your attention on the Moon during meditation you should think about your emotions and how they are forever changing. It is a chance to understand your dominant state feeling, the feeling that most often creeps up. It is a chance to understand your inner needs.

Mercury- Mercury relates to the mind, your perceptions and looking for fresh knowledge. You will learn how to communicate better, whether that's your ideas, your feelings, or your wishes.

Venus- this planet is linked to our hearts desires and our ability to give and receive love. You should be able to visualise this love filling you and those you care about. This will also bring forward our tastes and what we find pleasure from in life.

Mars- the root energy from Mars enables us to release energy and fulfil our most primal needs. We can meditate in order to express ourselves without inhibitions, to find our pure energy and motivation.

Jupiter- there is a level of understanding that allows us to appreciate the meaning of life. With Jupiter in our minds when we meditate, we can appreciate the opportunities that are given to us in life. We aim to improve our knowledge and wisdom.

Saturn- Saturn is associated with time and to some extent, how insignificant time is on the larger scale of things. Meditation will allow you to appreciate that the problems we suffer from now will not impact our lives in 5- or 10-years' time unless we allow them too.

There is a lot of information to consider and it does require a certain level of knowledge regarding the chakras, the planets (or Sun/Moon) and their different positions. You might be tempted to study all of what we have mentioned but that is a lot to digest, particularly as we still have plenty more to go.

My advice would be to look at your birth chart, understand when the heavenly bodies fall into the segments of your chakras and focus on the chakra that you would like to see an improvement. There is definitely time to work on all of your chakras but if you try to look at them all at the same time, you may discover it is difficult to visualise the specific chakra and meditate on the associated planet.

The next chapter is going to take a fascinating look at chakra massage and aromatherapy. We will also look at other techniques that can help balance our chakras, one in particular that has gained popularity in recent years.

CHAKRA MASSAGE AND AROMATHERAPY

E ven the words massage and aromatherapy are enough to bring a wave of calm over me and I have always felt that aromatherapy is never given the credit it deserves. We learnt about the importance of engaging all of our senses when we practice visualisation. Now, we are going to continue with this as we understand the significance of touch and smell while we work to balance our chakras.

CHAKRA MASSAGE

We have already looked at a few ways to unblock and create balance in our chakras from meditation to mantras and affirmations. Massage is another technique, especially for anyone who is new to chakra healing. Because the technique is relatively simple, you can do it yourself.

If you choose to go and see a massage therapist, I would strongly advise you to make sure they specialise in chakra massage and are well recommended. I worry so much that there are people giving our passion a bad name and trying to earn a quick buck, so I prefer to massage my own chakra areas.

Remember in the beginning how we said that a chakra isn't an organ or something we can see. We can't put our hands on a specific part of our body to start to awaken that chakra. Chakra massage involves movements and massage in areas of the body that are associated with the chakra. This massage carefully and correctly begins to awaken the chakra allowing the wheel to start spinning and the energy to flow.

For example, by massaging the muscles in your neck up towards the base of your skull and in a clockwise direction, you can begin to release energy in your Throat Chakra. When we dedicate each chapter to a different chakra, I will go into much more detail about massage techniques.

REFLEXOLOGY

Reflexology is an ancient Chinese healing technique based on a person's vital energy of Qi (pronounced 'chee'). Similar to the chakras, the Chinese believe that balance in this flow of energy is essential to help us stay free from disease and illnesses. Instead of focusing on the 7 chakras, reflexology refers to pressure points on the feet, hands, and ears.

That being said, there are correlations between the sole of the foot and the 7 chakras. This is because there are pressure points along the sole of the foot that stimulate specific nerves or glands. Now, I could go into all of the medical names for the parts of the body and you could look it up online, but where would the fun be in that! Why not take a piece of paper, draw around your left foot and then draw a vertical and horizontal line so that you have a cross right in the middle!

Slightly to the top of your cross and on the left-hand side, is the adrenal gland. Then, across the middle of your heel, there is a strip that is associated with the sciatic nerve. These two pressure points are related to the Root Chakra. Go on, you know you want to get your pens out and colour it red!!

For the Sacral Chakra, we need to move away from the sole of the foot temporarily. On the inside of your left foot, below and about one finger back, you will find the pressure point that is tied to the uterus or the prostate. On the outside of your right foot, in the same position below the ankle, there is the ovary or testicle pressure point. You could make a little note in orange.

Back to the sole for the Solar Plexus Chakra, and there are two pressure points. The first is just above the cross you drew, known as the solar plexus. The second starts on the inside of your left foot, just above the vertical line and spreads across almost to the horizontal line. These pressure points will be yellow.

Just next to the solar plexus pressure point, slightly higher and to the left, there is the heart pressure point. It is a larger area than the others, probably the size of your thumbprint. A little more to the left is the thymus gland. Dark green would be good but if not, green is fine.

Moving up the sole of the foot you will find the thyroid gland. This is located right under the joint of your big toe. You can colour this area blue.

Literally above the thyroid gland, there is a strip across the bottom of the big toe that is associated with the pituitary gland. This is linked to the Third Eye Chakra and should be coloured purple.

Finally, across the top of your big toe, there is the pressure point for the Crown Chakra. It is associated with the pineal gland. Imagine it like a painted tip of a toenail (but on the opposite side of the toe) and a lighter purple.

All of these pressure points have a mirror image when looking at your right foot. This is except for the Sacral Chakra which has specific left and right foot areas and the thumb-sized heart pressure point. This one is only found on the sole of the left foot.

I confess I am terrible with lefts and rights which is why I found it easier to draw my own feet and mark the different pressure points and if you use colours, not only can you gain from the frequency of the associated chakra colour, but it makes it easier to remember which nerve or gland is associated with each chakra. Again, I grabbed the first colours I can find. If you want to be more specific, you can pop back to chapter one.

Once you have identified the pressure point you would like to work with, you can apply pressure with your thumb for between 1 to 5 seconds and then release for 1 to 5 seconds. You can repeat this for up to 15 minutes. There are other techniques where the pressure is slowly increased and lasts for up to 60 seconds. This is usually only continued for up to 5 minutes.

There are plenty of benefits to reflexology. It can help to lower stress levels, alleviate pain and improve your mood. Furthermore, people have noticed improvements with digestion, nerve and arthritis pain and a boost in the immune system.

I consider myself to be a responsible spiritual healer and so I must warn you that if you have certain health concerns you should consult your doctor first. This includes circulatory problems in your feet, blood clots or inflammation in your legs, open wounds, foot ulcers or infections, thyroid problems or epilepsy. Also, consult a professional if you are pregnant. These pressure points may induce contractions.

REIKI

From Japan, Reiki is a healing technique that encompasses higher power and life force energy to get a spiritually guided life force energy. This energy is known as Ki, the Japanese version of the Chinese Qi. It is simple and as with the other methods we have looked at, it doesn't require any form of religious belief.

While you don't need to be religious in any way, you do need to be dedicated to seeing improvements in yourself. You also need to commit yourself to a virtuous life, so respectful, honest, and kind. This type of lifestyle is like the last link in completing the system and gaining the most healing value.

Healing from Reiki involves placing hands-on parts of the body to increase the life force energy within you. When carried out correctly, the benefits are amazing. You may notice improvements throughout your whole body from your emotions to your body, mind and spirit. It is incredibly relaxing, and the sense of peace is blissful.

With regards to our chakras, a Reiki master, or at least someone who has been trained by a Reiki master will place their hands on parts of the body that are associated with a particular chakra to help adjust the imbalances. Many of these body parts we have already talked about, but it is well worth a recap.

- **The Root Chakra-** adrenal glands, kidneys, spine, leg bones
- **The Sacral Chakra-** reproductive systems, spleen, bladder
- **The Solar Plexus Chakra-** pancreas, liver, stomach, spleen, lower digestive tract, gallbladder, autonomic nervous system

- **The Heart Chakra-** thymus gland, heart, circulatory system, lower lungs, hands, skin
- **The Throat Chakra-** thyroid gland, throat, jaw, upper lungs, vocal cords, upper digestive tract
- **Third Eye Chakra-** pituitary gland, lower brain, central nervous system, left eye, ears, nose
- **Crown Chakra-** pineal gland, upper brain, right eye

So, the only potential downside is that depending on your location, you may find it difficult to find a professional Reiki practitioner. However, Reiki education is becoming easier to find. In America, for example, Reiki education is offered in over 800 hospitals and for free.

On the upside, it is a simpler form of healing from your point of view as it is down to the expert to understand the exact locations of the healing areas. Perhaps the hardest part in today's world is living a virtuous life.

As well as an overall improvement in well-being, Reiki healing has been known to help alleviate pain, increase relaxation, reduce stress and anxiety and improve cognition in the elderly.

Thanks to the 'Center For Reiki Research', which was founded in 2005, more controlled, evidence-based research has been carried out compared with studies performed on reflexology. For this reason, Reiki might be seen as more credible and those who are interested in learning can find a Reiki master.

AROMATHERAPY

Am I the only one who smells the fabric softener and cleaning products in the supermarket before buying them? I love walking past the body shop, the smell of fresh-cut grass, puppies and bakeries. All of these smells have an effect on me that makes me smile. I close my eyes and breathe it all in!

Aromatherapy is the use of essential oils for healing, or at least to aid other healing techniques. Essential oils are (or at least should be) natural and are plant extracts taken from flowers, bark, leaves, or fruit. Various parts are steamed or pressed and then bottled.

When essential oils are breathed in, they are transported from the olfactory system to the brain. In the brain, certain smells will leave an impression on the amygdala, the part of the brain where we experience our emotions. This is why the smell of a Sunday roast can fill you with memories of happy family meals, etc.

Aromatherapy might not work for everyone as each person reacts differently to different smells. The air freshener in my husband's car makes me feel sick whereas freshly cut grass makes him sneeze. When used in the correct way they are perfectly safe and worth trying to see what benefit they have for you. Some studies have shown that they can help with anxiety, depression, insomnia, and nausea. If you are the type of person who is happier just from smelling coffee, it is likely that you will see some improvements in your mood alone.

Surprisingly, there are no regulations when it comes to labelling a bottle of essential oils and so because you can't be sure exactly what is in the bottle, essential oils should never be ingested. A few drops of peppermint essential oil in hot water doesn't make a peppermint tea.

Instead, an ideal way to gain from aromatherapy is to use wearable objects that are made of absorbent materials. I have a set of wooden mala beads which I use for mantras. It is perfect for rubbing in some essential oils and I can also use it as a bracelet or necklace. This may sound a bit girly, but the leather or rope wristbands will also work well.

Body oils are a combination of essential oils and other types of cream. These are wonderful for massages and as you can imagine, the perfect complement for chakra massage. You shouldn't use pure essential oils because they are concentrated, and you might find that the strength will irritate the skin. On that note, be careful of allergic reactions. Some people are allergic to cinnamon so can't eat it, but it is probable that they are allergic to cinnamon bark oil too, obviously, this is just one example.

When choosing essential oils, it is best not to go cheap- and this is coming from someone who loves a bargain! The cheaper brands may be mixed with chemicals so try to find labels that state 100% essential oils. It is also worth buying dark glass bottles because this helps retain the quality of the plant extracts.

Some of the most common essential oils are peppermint, tea tree and lavender. I bought a small wooden box because I knew I was going to end up with a good collection of bottles. Two birds with one stone, I also use the box to rub in the essential oils.

You may have guessed what I am about to say next! Each of our chakras responds to certain essential oils, helping you to find a better sense of balance. One that I had never heard of before was lime essential oil. It works wonders on helping you see the truth and straightening out the differences between fantasy and reality, therefore, it helps to create balance in your Crown Chakra. For the other chakras, I will explain more about specific essential oils in the following chapters.

Isn't it just amazing how many options you have? This is what is just so brilliant about chakras and alternative healing methods. You have so much potential to explore reflexology, massage, Reiki, and aromatherapy. If you feel that something doesn't suit you, it doesn't mean that you won't be able to create balance within your chakras, it just means you can experiment with other options.

I have tried everything that we have talked about so far. I'm not going to tell you my favourites because I don't want to influence you and to be honest, over the years I have discovered that certain options work better for certain situations. Mantras and affirmations, including the two-word expressions relating to the chakras, are best when used on a continuous basis. I like massage and reflexology when I feel that I need to destress, and aromatherapy works very well with both. Any opportunity that arises when I can learn from a Reiki master I am there! But there is no doubt that our senses can provide wonderful healing opportunities.

There are two more techniques of chakra healing that we are still going to talk about before an in-depth look at each chakra. One is more common, and you might even say socially accepted. The other may seem a little far out there for some but as with so many of the alternative healing approaches, I was captivated by the power of healing crystals.

CRYSTALS FOR BETTER INNER VIBRATIONS

When I first began writing books, I was told that I should try and leave myself out of it because really, the idea is to help you. But I strongly disagreed and went my own stubborn way. With a topic like spiritualism, I find it helps to include my side of things, especially considering how I started as a non-believer.

My first experience with crystals was way back in the nineties when I was close to finishing high school. A few of the cool kids started going on about how crystals were making them better people. First of all, in high school, our definition of a better person was somewhat mistaken and secondly, they had no idea of how they worked. Not wanting to go against the crowd, I carried a few around and as soon as the year was over, I vowed never to fall for "that rubbish again".

The second time someone insisted I try the powers of crystals I still lacked the confidence to say no thank you, and I remained cynical throughout.

Once I started to explore the Eastern Philosophies, I did recognise that I was becoming more open to trying new concepts, however, there was still something about crystals that I couldn't get my head around.

During my travels around India, I started to come around. In many parts of India, people can't afford modern medicine and therefore stick to the traditional healing methods, one of which was the use of crystals. Perhaps it was seeing them used in one of their original settings that made me feel like I could also learn how to use them to help with the balancing of my chakras.

HOW DO CRYSTALS HELP BALANCE YOUR CHAKRAS

When someone first told me that each crystal has a vibrational frequency, I was certainly not any more convinced. But it did start to make sense. Everything is still composed of energy; it is just the form and strength of energy that is different. The Vibration frequency of crystals will depend on the material, thickness and needless to say, their colour.

To an extent, the science behind crystals and healing is all about understanding the vibration frequencies of each stone and how this will help with particular chakras. Thankfully, crystal healing has also been around for thousands of years, and so the trial and error has been done for us. And because of this, so many people have been able to benefit from gemstones and crystals when awakening and balancing their chakras.

You know by now that crystals and gemstones of a certain colour are going to be associated with each of the chakras. While you might be tempted to choose a crystal that you relate to your chakras- like a particular tone of red, crystals that have the same shades will also work well. What is more important is to look at the particular attributes and energetic qualities as well as feeling a connection to that crystal or gemstone.

Take for example clear quartz. It's like the "Om" of crystal healing, the master that can often be paired with other crystals to enhance their healing benefits. It can increase energy levels, even help to store it and release it when necessary. It is perfect for creating balance across the whole body and may even help with concentration. I have clear raw quartz in my crystal cluster but it's not one of my personal go-to crystals. I prefer those that are smoother, have been polished and have elements of colour. I still believe in its qualities and use it when the time is right, but you need to be drawn to the crystals you choose.

A bit like our essential oils, there are a few crystals that are great to include at the beginning of your collection, and I wanted to quickly look at these before we focus on our chakras.

Blue lace agate- part of the quartz family, this is a light blue stone with soft darker blue bands across it. It can help lower your levels of anxiety and enable you to absorb its calming energy.

Selenite- this is a crystallised form of Gypsum and is very powerful in spiritual healing. It can assist in clearing your energy field and especially useful if you have to deal with other people's negativity.

Pyrite- also known as Fool's Gold because of its colour, pyrite is also used in Feng Shui for attracting wealth. For healing, it can help us to remind you of how full your life is.

Shungite- this is yet to be proven by scientists, but this stone might be able to counterbalance the electromagnetic frequencies which are more and more part of our daily lives.

Black tourmaline- it can be quite rough or beautifully smooth when polished. Black tourmaline can be used for an overall layer of spiritual protection. It can help to ground your energies as well as protect them.

Just to give you a little taster of the different crystals, you can find one for each of the associated chakras, but I don't recommend buying this one straight away. When we focus on the chakras individually, we will look at more crystals and gemstones that you might prefer.

- Root Chakra- Fire Agate
- Sacral Chakra- Coral
- Solar Plexus Chakra- Topaz
- Heart Chakra- Jade
- Throat Chakra- Aquamarine
- Third Eye Chakra- Amethyst
- Crown Chakra- Clear Quartz

USING CRYSTALS TO BALANCE YOUR CHAKRAS

Crystals and gemstones are ready to be used but if you want to gain the most from their energies, they need to be programmed with your needs and intentions. It's like when you buy a new phone, you have all of the hardware there ready, but you need to download the right apps for you. The phone will still work without your favourite apps but with them, you will get more out of the phone.

To program your crystals, you need to know exactly how you want them to work. If you have a fire agate, you will want to hold your crystal in your hands, close your eyes and relax. Focus your attention on your crystal and the Root Chakra. Then you need to say aloud or in your head a sentence that shows a commitment to your stone. Examples of these sentences may include:

- I will work with this crystal to create balance in my Root Chakra
- I will work with this crystal to take more control over my life
- I will feel the vibrations of my crystal and find more peace

Finish off with a meaningful thank you. You will need to do the same for each of your crystals repeating a sentence that is appropriate for the intentions and goals of that stone. Now that each of your crystals is programmed you can explore some of the best ways to use them. Don't forget that you don't have to stick to just one use, feel free to combine them as you see fit and in a way that can be incorporated into your daily lives.

1. Wearing your crystals

The more contact you can have with your crystal, the more energy you will be able to absorb from it. The popularity of crystals has encouraged a whole new fashion where crystals are part of the clothing design. You can also wear jewellery with your crystal. Because I was still a little dubious at first, I found an ideal solution was to search for rings with my crystal and program it before wearing it.

This might all sound a bit girly but there are plenty of more masculine solutions for jewellery that contain crystals and gemstones. An alternative option is to make your own.

2. Keep them in a purse or pocket

They may be out of sight but not out of mind. Knowing that your crystals are still close to you throughout the day means you can still hold them at regular intervals. Pockets are great, especially if you have a habit of keeping your hands in them.

3. Hold them while you meditate

Meditation is a way to feel a closer connection with your spiritual energy and with yourself. Holding a crystal while you meditate will further strengthen this connection. For added benefit, you can program your crystal to match the intention of your meditation.

4. A crystal layout

Once you have a crystal for each of your chakras, you can lay down and place each one on your chakra, so you would start by placing your fire agate on your Root Chakra and continue up along your spine. This is perfect for gaining a complete sensation of energy. Rest there for 5 minutes while you focus on your breathing.

5. Add them to the tub with your favourite bubble bath

The bath is a great way to combine crystal with aromatherapy for complete relaxation along with the combined intention of your crystal. Make sure that your crystal is one that is suitable for use in water.

6. Include them in your decor

The crystals you have should be those that you are attracted to so it makes sense that you place them around your home. You can admire their beauty and cleanse the energy in your home. This is logically the best option for the larger crystals that may look a bit stupid sticking out of your pocket or hanging around your neck.

7. Sleep near your crystals

Whether on the bedside table or under your pillow, you can gain from the energy of the crystal while you are asleep. Hold your crystal while you lay in bed, take a few deep breaths and imagine the energies of your crystal.

THE THREE CS OF CRYSTAL CARE

Just like the phone we originally programmed; our crystals need to be taken care of. This requires cleansing, clearing, and charging them so that they continue to provide us with the energies, support, and healing that we are working towards.

Cleansing

Your crystal has already had its own journey before arriving in your hands. As we aren't sure what has happened to it along the way, we need to cleanse it to remove any possible negative energies.

Before programming your crystals, run them under a tap with cool water. If you can, take them to a river or a source of naturally flowing water. Adding salt to the water will enhance the cleansing, so seawater is perfect. Some people like to burn sage too.

These physical acts are only one part of the cleansing. You need to mentally remove any negative energies, especially those coming from you. Replace any doubts you may have with respect for their abilities.

Clearing

Crystal energy works both ways. As we absorb the benefits of their energies, they also absorb the energies around them. It is important to clear your crystals, particularly if you are going through an incredibly stressful time, if you have had an argument with someone, or if you have been ill.

You can clear your crystals the same way as you cleansed them when you first got them. Either run them under the tap or wash them in a natural source of water, using salt and smoke from sage to help remove the negative energies they might have absorbed. Don't forget that not all crystals can be submerged in water and for some, you can only use smoke.

· · ·

Charging

Everything that requires energy requires charging from our electrical devices to our own bodies. Here are some ways for you to charge your crystals:

The Moon- placing your crystals under the moonlight, especially a full moon, will recharge your crystals with feminine energy and can help us with our spiritual and emotional healing.

The sun- we know how energised we feel when the sun is out. Placing your crystals in direct sunlight allows them to take in the masculine solar energy, which may help you for those occasions that require a big effort from your behalf.

Earth- burying your crystal in the earth for up to 24 hours can recharge it with energies from nature and nearby plants.

Use other crystals- create a circle with your other crystals and place the crystal to be charged in the middle. Again, you should probably leave the crystal circle for at least 24 hours.

Use your own energy- If you feel that you are buzzing with positive energy, lay your crystals out in front of you and focus your energy on the crystals. I like to think of this as giving a little back!

CHOOSING THE RIGHT CRYSTALS FOR YOU

There are more than 4,000 different types of crystals on our planet. You may find one crystal has specific attributes that you think will benefit you, then the following website will tell you that it has other energetic powers. Neither one may be wrong, in fact, one crystal may have different meanings associated with it.

With so many to choose from it can feel a little overwhelming when you first begin, especially if you have walked into an alternative healing shop and seen all of the options. You can buy a set but there is one big risk with this; you may fall in love with a few of them, but not all of them. Your crystals have to speak to you, you have to choose them and not accept what comes in a pack.

Don't get me wrong, some of the sets available are beautiful and are absolutely perfect, just be careful if you are buying them online.

Use your intuition. Rather than searching for crystals based on your chakras, choose ones that you like the feel of and the colours appeal to you. No crystal will be wrong for you or do you harm because you are going to cleanse it and program it with your own intentions.

Also bear in mind that although crystals have great energy, they won't perform miracles. You won't wake up after 24 hours and feel like a completely new person. A good rule of thumb is to keep your crystal with you for 30 days. After this time and you don't feel any different, you can try a different crystal, always remembering to cleanse, program and when necessary, clear and charge them.

Entire books are dedicated to crystal healing so you can understand that one chapter really is just the introduction. As I keep promising, you will learn more about specific crystals for each chakra once we have looked into the amazing practice of yoga, the different kinds of yoga and how they can not only strengthen our body but also optimise the balancing process.

YOGA: YOUR ULTIMATE SELF

Oh, Yoga how I love you! For myself, and so many others, yoga was our first introduction to the spiritual world without even realising it. I started practising yoga before I ever found an interest in other spiritual practices. In my early days, I loved yoga for stretching and I felt myself getting physically stronger. I enjoyed the step away from the buzz of the outside world and a chance to take in the peace.

THE ORIGIN OF YOGA

Mantras were first mentioned in the ancient Hindi scriptures, the Upanishads and we know that the teaching of mantras was predominantly orally, which has allowed for some differences in interpretations. Yoga also dates back to more than 5,000 years ago from the Indus-Saraswati civilisation in Northern India.

The first mention of yoga was also in the Upanishads, but some believe the practice might be as old as 10,000 years.

I am going to assume that you don't know that yoga has 4 key historical periods and I will briefly mention them. Some may not be interested in the history of yoga and that is absolutely fine. I have always appreciated the research and knowledge so that I can have more respect for the Eastern Philosophies and how they came about.

Pre-Classical Yoga

The Vedas, the sacred Hindu texts, were used by Vedic priests, or Brahmans and. Yoga was thought to have begun as a ritual sacrifice. Brahmans, along with Rishis (Indian spiritual masters) then developed the concept of yoga into a style of teaching that encouraged the sacrifice of the ego through karma yoga and jnana yoga, action and wisdom respectively. At this point, there was no clear definition of what yoga was, it was more of a combination of different beliefs and methods.

Classical Yoga

In the second century CE, yoga became more systematic thanks to Patanjali's Yoga-Sutras. The Yoga-Sutras have a great influence on today's yoga practices and Patanjalios description of the path of Raja Yoga is still known as classical yoga.

Post-Classical Yoga

Skip ahead a few more centuries and yoga masters were beginning to create systems that were not related to Vedas but instead, on ways to rejuvenate the body. In this period, the masters formed Tantra Yoga, based on the idea of cleansing the body and the mind. It was used to explore the connections we have between the spiritual and physical world, which led to what we know as Hatha Yoga.

Modern Yoga

This leads us to the yoga we practise today. From the late 1800s, yoga masters began travelling West. Books were written and yoga centres began popping up all over the world. The varieties of Hatha Yoga include yoga postures (asanas), yoga breathing (pranayama), internal cleansing (shatkarma), and life-force energy (prana). Most of today's yoga focuses on yoga postures.

There are two forms of yoga that can catch our attention when looking to balance our chakras, Chakra Yoga and Kundalini Yoga.

REACHING YOUR POTENTIAL WITH CHAKRA YOGA

Regardless of our previous yoga experience, we can all appreciate the benefits of a good stretch. First thing in the morning or after a few hours of sitting at the desk, a stretch helps us to loosen the muscles that have tightened after lack of activity. Stretching increases blood flow to our muscles.

Now when you combine the stretching we do with certain yoga poses with controlled breathing, we are able to increase the amount of oxygen that flows throughout our entire body. It is a successful method for cleansing the body and encouraging a balance among our chakras. The postures used in Chakra Yoga involve keeping your body aligned and specifically your spine straight, allowing the energy to flow more easily to each chakra.

Some people will incorporate meditation into Chakra Yoga. You can increase your focus and sharpen your mind at the same time as awakening your chakras. Let's take a brief look at a couple of yoga poses that will benefit each chakra.

The Root Chakra

Here, we are looking to create more power around the area that keeps us grounded, the pelvic floor muscles. The Warrior Pose stretches out our hips and the Chair Pose strengthens the hip flexors.

The Sacral Chakra

If you can see this chakra as the centre of your fluids from sweat, blood to tears, this chakra being awakened will encourage flow and fluidity in the rest of your body. It is also advised to work on hip-opening poses such as the bound and open-angle poses.

The Solar Plexus Chakra

This can be seen as the home of your potential power and vitality. Yoga poses that involve twists will help to experience the energy in this chakra. Some of the simpler poses include the Triangle Pose and the Half Lord of the Fishes Pose.

The Heart Chakra

As the Heart Chakra is the meeting of our lower and higher chakras, the poses should create harmony between the body and the spirit. Backbends awaken the Heart Chakra, allowing the energy to enhance our compassion and feel more secure about ourselves.

The Throat Chakra

The Plow and the Camel Yoga poses are good for stretching the back and shoulders. On top of this, the Camel pose expands the stomach area and encourages energy up towards the throat.

The Third Eye Chakra

The place where the body meets the mind, healing can include Nadi Shodhana or alternate nostril breathing. In terms of yoga poses, the cat-cow pose strengthens the neck and the spine helps to reduce stress and can encourage emotional balance.

The Crown Chakra

The higher up the chakras, the more we work towards our spiritual connections. For this reason, meditation is one of the best ways to encourage energy to the Crown Chakra. You can also practise the Half Lotus pose that goes nicely with meditation.

Another reason to love yoga is that you don't need anything. If you want to join a class to really master the techniques, there are classes available at all times of the day and for all different levels.

That being said, not everyone can squeeze a full class into their daily routine. Fitness games on computers like the Wii and the Nintendo Switch have very sophisticated Yoga "games" that allow you to practice particular poses or even create your own routine, whether that's just for a couple of poses before you start your day or even 15 to 20 mins. There is plenty of flexibility in creating your own yoga routine.

A BLENDED APPROACH WITH KUNDALINI YOGA

Despite sounding like a type of pasta, Kundalini Yoga goes hand in hand with the balancing of chakras. The West was introduced to Kundalini Yoga in the 1970s, but its exact date of origin is unknown.

Kundalini Yoga concentrates on the energy that sits at the base of our spine. Through breathing, movement, and sound, we are able to tap into this energy and encourage this energy to flow up through our 7 chakras.

Kundalini Shakti- meaning Serpent Power

The snake has powerful imagery, first as the inactive energy is seen as 'coiled energy' and second, the process of Kundalini Yoga is a transformation of oneself, just as a snake would shed its old skin.

There have been enough scientific studies to demonstrate the health benefits of Kundalini Yoga. A study in 2018 showed that it can help to reduce the symptoms of anxiety disorders while another in 2017 showed a decrease in cortisol levels and perceived stress. Some of the other health benefits may include:

- Toned muscles
- A boost in your mood
- Lower blood pressure and heart rate
- Better focus
- Faster metabolism
- Improved digestion

The good news is that we have already covered the three core aspects of Kundalini Yoga, breathing, mantras, and poses. The last thing for us to do before we probe into each individual chakra is to see how our breathing, mantras, and poses relate specifically to Kundalini Yoga.

Breathing

There are specific types of controlled breathing for each action performed in this type of yoga and each one is controlled and focused. Some are long deep breaths and others, like the favoured Breath of Fire, is short and fast.

The Breath of Fire requires fast equal breaths in through the nose and out through the nose and out through the nose. This encourages the lungs to act as a pump for oxygen to be pushed around the body and charge the electromagnetic field around you.

Mantras

Mantras use the power of specific sound vibrations to channel energy to either specific chakras, or for all over energy flow. These vibrations have a way of making a person feel better by increasing positivity and lifting the mood.

In chapter 3, we looked at the 7 bija or seed mantras for each of the chakras and we will revise them in part 3. I also wanted to look at some other popular mantras that are used for Kundalini Yoga in general.

"Har" but it can also be Hara or Hari- Creative infinity

"Hari Nam, Sat Nam Hari Nam, Hari.
Hari Nam, Sat Nam, Sat Name, Hari"- The name of God is the True Name

"Ong So Hung"- Creator, I am Thou
"Hum Dum Har Har"- We the inverse, God, God"

Don't forget that you don't need to practice any religion to benefit from mantras. Although they are often considered types of prayers, it is the vibrations that we are gaining from. If you don't feel comfortable with these mantras, the bija mantras are only sounds rather than having any religious vocabulary, it's a personal choice.

Poses

These yoga poses when combined with breathing and mantras are known as Kriyas. There are thousands of Kriyas and it all goes back to your intention. Here is an example of one of the basic ones.

The Ego Eradicator

Pose- Sit in the Easy Pose with legs crossed and spine straight, lift your arms straight out to a 60° angle, curl your fingertips in and raise your thumbs up. Close your eyes.

Breathing- Breath of Fire, short equal breaths through the nose

Mantra- "Ma" and keep your focus on the area above your head

You can do the Ego Eradicator for 1 to 3 minutes before you get up in the morning and if you feel it is necessary, you can extend it for up to 6 minutes. It is an ideal Kriya for opening your lungs, feeling more mentally alert, and uniting your magnetic field.

You should be clear on your healing intentions by name. Still, it is widely agreed that the primary goal of Kundalini Yoga is to push your life force energy up from its coiled position, through the chakras. Once it has reached the crown chakra, you are able to appreciate enlightenment.

Needless to say, this will take some dedication. If you are already comfortably using some mantras, you can incorporate these into your Kundalini Yoga. You can also combine this with aromatherapy and have your crystals nearby if this is what you feel is right.

The power of the mind, focus, dedication, and a genuine belief in your chakra energy and balance are the key things that need to remain consistent. The rest are tools and techniques that you should enjoy exploring.

With so many different things to try, consider keeping a journal to make a note of the techniques you have tried and how you have felt afterwards. This will allow you to narrow down the best methods that work for you gradually. I love looking back at my journal and it inspires me to try things again to see the new impact after gaining more experience.

PART III
A STEP-BY-STEP GUIDE TO BALANCING CHAKRAS

The time has finally come, and this part of the book needs little introduction! The next 7 chapters will each cover one of the 7 chakras. We will review what we have already learnt about them in terms of the associated body parts and emotions. We will delve deeper into what to expect in the process of awakening and balancing chakras.

The techniques we have been over have been quite general so far, but now is the moment that we work on choosing the precise crystals and essential oils as well as massage techniques for the associated body parts.

There will be some new mantras and affirmations to try and a few other meditation tips. Finally, rather than naming yoga poses and Kriyas, I am going to use my creative side to describe how to perform these powerful actions.

Many people believe that earth itself has its own chakras. To complete our understanding of chakras, I will tell you a little more about each of these. My goal in life is to visit them all, but the few that I have been to have allowed an incredible connection to the different chakras.

I am so excited to be taking this final step of the journey with you, so let's make it a memorable one.

AWAKENING THE ROOT CHAKRA

L et's begin by reviewing what we have covered so far in terms of the location of the Root Chakra and what symptoms may be experienced when it is blocked. Up to now, we have only used the English name, but it is called the Muladhara Chakra. The first of the seven chakras is located at the base of our spine.

It's the closest chakra to earth and is tied to our sense of being grounded. It is the support and foundation for our lives. It is related to feeling safe and secure, as well as our basic needs such as food, sleep, and a place to live.

Red is the colour linked to the Root Chakra. It is appropriate as this chakra is the densest of the seven and red is the densest of all the chakras. Red has the slowest wavelengths, but it is also an extremely stimulating colour that draws our focus and attention.

Your Root Chakra is associated with your legs, feet, ankles, bladder, and the large intestine, adrenal glands.

Here is a quick guide to the physical and emotional symptoms associated with the Root Chakra:

- Physical symptoms when blocked: the inability to sit still, weakness in the legs, overweight, kidney stones, circulatory issues.
- Physical symptoms when overactive: bladder issues, constipation, fatigue, anaemia.
- Emotional symptoms when blocked: it is likely that you will feel insecure about life and even anger. I describe it as the feeling when you have itchy feet and can't find a way to settle yourself.
- An overactive Root Chakra: your basic needs aren't being met and this leads you to feel threatened, bringing about anxiety and fear.
- An underactive Root Chakra: you may live in a dreamland and far from grounded. It could be that you have never had to worry about the basic things in life.

When your Root Chakra is balanced you will feel happy and comfortable within yourself and your environment, like you belong. You are able to appreciate your body and your place in the world. Above all, you feel in control of your life.

HOW TO HEAL A BLOCKED ROOT CHAKRA

HEALING THROUGH SOUND

The bija mantra, or seed mantra, for the Root Chakra is "Lam", a deep sound that will help to clear blockages and encourage energy to start flowing up to the other chakras. By chanting Lam 108 times you should start to feel less worried and more grounded. The English version (not the translation) is "I am".

There are also several affirmations that can help to unblock and create balance in this chakra. While you can still make up your own affirmations, I wanted to give you a little inspiration with words that are related to a connection to the earth.

- I am grounded
- I am standing with my feet firmly on the ground
- I am safe
- Like the trees and the stars, I have the right to be here
- I trust myself
- I feel the good in life

AWAKENING THE ROOT CHAKRA WITH VISUALISATION AND MEDITATION

In Northern California, you can find Mount Shasta. This active volcano has a breath-taking and spiritual presence surrounded by natural beauty, forests and meadows. Many see Mount Shasta as the Root Chakra of Earth's energy and native American's worship this volcano, believing it is the centre of the Universe.

The connection between the planet Mars and the colour red is no coincidence. Meditating while visualising this planet will help to draw in its energies. It is wise to meditate outside where you can be in closer contact with the earth. I like to lay down on the grass, but you might prefer to sit on the ground or at least, sit on a chair with your feet placed firmly on the ground to help you feel rooted.

Take long slow deep breaths and imagine the energy of Mars and your astrological sign filling each part of your body. You can visualise this energy as a light that passes into your lungs and spreads all the way down to your toes. If you are laying on the ground, you may feel the light in a complete circle around you, a link between your body and the ground.

Each breath should fill you with warmth and comfort like you are being embraced but it should also make you feel empowered, strong, and give you a sense of belonging.

Don't forget to express your gratitude to Mars before and after your meditation.

YOGA AND REIKI FOR YOUR ROOT CHAKRA

For our yoga poses, we should practice Sukhasana (Easy Pose), Malasana (Garland Pose) and Virabhadrasana II (Warrior II).

Easy Pose- Sitting down with crossed legs, tilt your pelvis forward slightly so that your spine is completely straight. As you sit on the ground, breath in the energy from the earth and breathe out any negativity or anxiety you may feel.

Garland Pose- The best way to describe this is like you are taking a pee in the countryside! Squat down low with your feet pointed out at an angle. Tuck your elbows into your knees and keep your hands in the prayer position. This is another pose that keeps you close to the ground and can strengthen your lower back, hips, claves, and ankles.

Warrior II- Stand with your legs spread as far as possible while being comfortable. Keep one foot in the same position while you turn the other 90° clockwise with your knee facing in the same direction. Your arms are raised to a 90° angle with the tips of your fingers stretching in opposite directions in line with your body. Repeat the same in the opposite direction. Warrior II helps us with our flight or fight response and enables us to face our fears.

For Reiki healing, lay down and feel the stretch in your spine, lay your hands over the very tops of your legs so that they are covering the lower pelvic area. Massaging your gluteus maximus, gluteus medius, and gluteus minimus (that's your bum and outer hip muscles to us laymen) will help to relieve tension around your Root Chakra. You can also massage and stretch all of the muscles in your legs.

AROMATHERAPY AND CRYSTAL HEALING

Frankincense has a fresh clean smell and can help slow down the breathing when meditating. Patchouli offers clarity and allows you to enjoy the present moment by yourself, it may even help you to focus and reach your goals. Cedarwood is another one of my favourites because it has a very calming effect and a real scent of nature.

Red crystals, in general, are going to be of great help for creating balance in your Root Chakra whether that's to keep them on you or for visualisation during meditation. Some others that I have used are:

- Black Tourmaline- this semi-precious black stone is used to help keep us grounded.
- Red Jasper- it is a deep earthy red colour and it reminds me of the power Mars has and it will help to cleanse and balance.
- Bloodstone- I love the dark green colour with the

speckles of red. You can wear this to increase your self-esteem and protect yourself from negativity.

- Red Carnelian- the lighter red, almost orange appearance can give you strength and courage, particularly useful for the flight or fight instinct.

By using just one of these techniques, you will start to see a difference. Once you have explored different methods to awaken your Root Chakra and decided on the best choices for you, you will soon start to feel balance as your energy begins to flow up towards the Sacral Chakra.

AWAKENING THE SACRAL CHAKRA

You will also hear the Sacral Chakra being called Svadhisthana and is the second chakra as we move up our spine. We associate the Sacral Chakra with the pleasure we are able to experience through our senses. It lets us feel the world around us and can create flexibility in our lives. It plays a significant role in our sex life including the ability to express our sexual desires.

Orange is the colour that is tied to our Sacral Chakra, more specifically, a transparent and almost transparent orange. Because of the associate of water, the Sacral chakra may take on a light blue colour.

The Sacral Chakra can impact our reproductive system, the ovaries, testes, and uterus. It might also cause problems with our kidneys when unbalanced. Let's revise some of the other symptoms associated with a blocked Sacral Chakra.

- **Physical symptoms when blocked:** Lower back pain and stiffness in this area is quite common. People may experience urinary problems, kidney pain and/or infections. Impotence or infertility may even be present.

- **Physical symptoms when overactive:** As well as the above mentioned, you might suffer from cysts and bladder issues. The excess energy in your Sacral Chakra can cause warmth in your lower abdomen area.

- **An overactive Sacral Chakra:** Emotions could be running high, you might experience mood swings or become overly sensitive, dependant, or obsessive.

- **An underactive Sacral Chakra:** You may fear pleasure and be generally insecure. The lack of energy can make you feel tired and without desire or inspiration.

When you start to bring balance to your Sacral Chakra, you will feel like you have complete control of your emotions. You will be confident and generous, and you will be fully aware of personal boundaries. As you can imagine, you will also be able to enjoy positively exploring your sexuality.

HEALING THROUGH SOUND

Focus on the area around three fingers below your navel. Repeat the bija mantra "Vam" in multiples of 108. In English, you can repeat the words "I feel" while concentrating on your various feelings and senses. Don't forget what you can hear and smell.

For affirmations to help awaken and balance the Sacral Chakra, you can choose one of the following or even combine them if you prefer. For added impact, start your Sacral Chakra affirmation with "I feel".

- I feel joy inside me
- My life is happy
- Creativity flows through my body
- I celebrate my sexuality
- I deserve pleasure and passion
- I have faith in my feelings

AWAKENING THE SACRAL CHAKRA WITH VISUALIZATION AND MEDITATION

It makes sense that a large body of water is the Sacral Chakra of the earth. Lake Titicaca in Peru and Bolivia is home to 'Isla del Sol', Island of the Sun and makes for a stunning image of orange and light blue.

Meditation is a wonderful way to become more attuned to your emotions and allow all of your feelings to flow. I like to imagine my emotions attaching themselves to the energy spinning in my Sacral chakra and then passing around my body.

It is best to meditate while sitting down with your hips higher than your knees. Loosen the sacral area by tilting your pelvis back and forward a few times and then completely relax your lower back and hips.

Though Venus is the planet that is linked to our Sacral Chakra, many people will use the sun as part of visualisation due to its bright orange appearance. Imagine the sun setting over the ocean. Breath in as the waves roll in and out as they drift back. Take in the colour of the sun and its ray reflect on the water. Absorb its vibrancy and focus this energy on your Sacral Chakra. To stimulate your senses, you can play the sound of the ocean while you meditate.

YOGA AND REIKI FOR YOUR ROOT CHAKRA

The following poses can help to increase the energy in your Sacral Chakra, but they can also release any excess energy you may have, causing an overactive chakra. The Utkata Konasana (Goddess Pose), Prasarita Padottanasana C (Wide-Legged Forward Bend C), and Supta Baddha Konasana (Reclined Bound Angle Pose) poses work towards opening your hips and filling you with the confidence to experience a fulfilling life.

Goddess Pose- Stand like the New Zealand Rugby team do when they are about to perform the Haka, hips wide open, knees bent, feet turned outwards, and slowly sink down. Keep your spine straight and place your palms together in front of your heart.

Wide-Legged Forward Bend C- This is one of the best stretches for your body and I love it, but please take care not to lose your balance! While standing up, spread your legs as far as you can and keep your feet facing forward. Link your fingers behind your back and rest them on the base of your spine. Slowly roll your neck, then shoulders and spine down so you are looking through your legs. Push your hips forward as you gradually move your hands away from your spine towards the floor.

Reclined Bound Angle Pose- Lie down with your knees bent and your feet together flat on the floor. Let your knees fall to the ground as the soles of your feet touch. You can stretch the spine more by crossing your arms above your head or you can practice Reiki by placing your palms on your Sacral Chakra.

Like the Root Chakra, chakra massage is focused on those bum muscles again, but you can also concentrate on the iliopsoas muscles, those that run from the lower spine to the pelvis.

AROMATHERAPY AND CRYSTAL HEALING

I found that Clary Sage is perfect for giving yourself an emotional uplift and as the name suggests, it will help to clarify how you are feeling. Orange oil can stimulate the liver as well as your creativity. And to increase your sex drive, Ylang Ylang and its aphrodisiac qualities may help your relationship.

For the crystals, amber and citrine are good stones to keep for the visual aspect. Others closely related to Sacral Chakra healing include:

- Orange and coral calcite- This stone can be used for cleansing and it is also a good crystal for distance healing.
- Orange Carnelian- If you are in an abusive relationship, this stone may help you overcome the abuse. It can also restore vitality and help to calm an overactive Sacral Chakra.
- Orange Adventurine- To unblock your Sacral Chakra and inspire your imagination and creativity, keep Orange Adventurine close by.
- Tiger's Eye- The stone of the mind can be dark and golden to yellow. It can help you to understand your emotions and make clearer decisions.

Not having control over your emotions or experiencing extremes such as depression or isolation is a very sad and difficult way to live life. It is amazing what just a few minutes a day can do to change your outlook on life for the better. Whether it's wearing a crystal in a piece of jewellery or starting your day with a bija mantra, you too can start to see a change.

AWAKENING THE SOLAR PLEXUS CHAKRA

The Manipura or Solar Plexus Chakra is located above the Sacral Chakra where your diaphragm is. It can influence the way we view ourselves in society and help us to find our path in life. The energy found in the Solar Plexus Chakra helps us to find momentum and action so that we can create ideas which then lead us to realise our dreams.

We have seen that the Solar Plexus Chakra is yellow but as this Chakra's element is fire, it can often be a golden, firefly yellow much like the sun. It also connected to the heat and energy produced by the sun.

Suppose you have noticed problems with your digestive system whether that's the stomach or intestines. In that case, you may have a blocked Sacral Chakra. It is also associated with the central nervous system, the liver, pancreas, and the metabolic system.

Physical symptoms when blocked: You might experience ulcers, gas, nausea, eating disorders or even respiratory problems like asthma. Liver or kidney infections may be related to the Solar Plexus Chakra and even nerve pain or fibromyalgia.

Emotional symptoms when blocked: People often feel as though they lack purpose. They can obsess over the tiny details of life and can't see the whole picture. You may find it important to have complete control over everything or the other extreme is a sense of helplessness.

An overactive Solar Plexus Chakra: When overactive, you might come across as dominating to the point of aggression. It is easy to criticise yourself too much and those around you.

An underactive Solar Plexus Chakra: You will tend to be passive in most situations. It is hard for you to make choices and you will often be quite timid.

You will be able to assert yourself when your Solar Plexus Chakra is balanced. This helps you to get what you want without having to overexert yourself. The balance you experience spreads to your relationships.

HEALING THROUGH SOUND

The vibrations created with the bija mantra Ram should be drawn towards your Solar Plexus Chakra, imaging the energy flowing up your spine towards your diaphragm. Focus on the colour yellow filling your body.

The words "I do" can be very empowering. As a blocked Solar Plexus Chakra can impede our ability to create ideas and carry them out, I find that the words "I do" reminds me that I am able to develop ways to do what I want to do.

Some affirmations that you can use throughout the day or as part of your morning routine are:

- I am capable of achieving my dreams
- I am valuable
- I am confident I have the skills to succeed
- I know what is best for myself
- I do not need to control
- I use my power for good

AWAKENING THE SOLAR PLEXUS CHAKRA WITH VISUALIZATION AND MEDITATION

Some cultures see the Solar Plexus Chakra as the house of the soul. The Earth's Solar Plexus Chakra is two rocks about 18 miles apart, Kata Tjuta and Uluru in Australia. Looking at these giant rocks I get a sense of both security and power.

Nobody can deny the power of the sun! When there is a break in those cold rainy days and the sky is lit with this ball of power, we walk with an extra bounce in our step, and we smile.

It's important to make the most of the sun so we can meditate outside. Go for a short walk, or even just around your garden a few times to get the body moving. Sit down and face the sun with your palms open towards the sun. Relax, breathe and feel the warmth surround you. Believing in the power of the sun will enable you to do this indoors or during the darker, colder months. Visualise the sun and the warmth on your face, moving across your body towards your fingertips and all the way down to your toes.

Every now and again I like to go to a park or sit in the country-side early in the morning. No technology, no distractions, just peace. I sit down and watch the sunrise. I empty my mind of everything and literally just spend 20 minutes watching the sun in admiration. The connection with nature and the tranquillity helps me to feel in control and more determined.

YOGA AND REIKI FOR YOUR ROOT CHAKRA

To increase the energy flow to our Solar Plexus Chakra, you can try Virabhadrasana I (Warrior I), Navasana (Boat Pose), and Parivrtta Anjaneyasana (Revolved Crescent Lunge.

Warrior I- Stand with your legs spread as wide as you can, turn to one side so your feet and body are pointing in the same direction. Lower the stretch as you bend your knee, placing more weight on this front leg. Reach your arms towards the sky.

Half Boat Pose- This requires a good level of balance. Begin by sitting down with your knees bent and feet flat on the floor. Keep your spine straight and raise your knees. There should be a straight line from your shoulder, through your arms, knees and down to your ankles. The full-boat pose requires your hands taking the tips of your toes as you sit in a V shape.

Revolved Crescent Lunge- from Warrior I, drop your chest towards your knees. Now, if your left knee is bent, take your right elbow and place it on the outside of the right knee. Keep your gaze forward as you put your hands together in the prayer position. Hold for 5 seconds and repeat on the other side.

Massaging the Solar Plexus is very simple to do yourself. Start by laying on the floor and place your hands on your diaphragm. Feel for warmth for a few minutes. In a clockwise direction rub 10 circles over your stomach, don't feel the need to rush this and don't worry about those "softer" bits of belly. Don't tense your muscles just to try and hide a little fat.

AROMATHERAPY AND CRYSTAL HEALING

Geraniums are lovely flowers and the essential oil is like loveliness in a bottle, it can help lower anxiety. Juniper Berry can be used internally to improve kidney function. Cypress oil has a lovely evergreen smell as if you are walking through the woods and it has been known to help with respiratory problems.

Some ideas for healing crystals could be:

Mookaite- this is a very special stone that is only found in Australia, so I love it for the connection to Uluru and Kata Tjuta. The golden, yellow, and tones of rich red had strong connections to the earth's electromagnetic current.

Lemon Quartz- when you catch the light on lemon quartz it can be compared to the rays of the sun. It is known for its ability to promote optimism.

Yellow Tourmaline- it can look very similar to Lemon Quartz, but Yellow Tourmaline can be used to help cleanse and detoxify the body.

Yellow Jasper- aside for helping bring balance to the Solar Plexus, it can also offer you protection.

The Solar Plexus Chakra is the last of the three lower chakras, those that are related to our Ego, our insecurities and our fears. The next chakra is the Heart Chakra, the connection between the lower and higher chakras or the body and the mind.

AWAKENING THE HEART CHAKRA

The connection between our higher and lower chakras, the Heart Chakra is essential for emotional development and unconditional love. Also known as the Anahata, the Heart Chakra sits in the middle of the chest, though some feel it is more to the left, just above the heart. As well as joining the higher and lower chakras, the body and the mind, it also links the earth world to the spiritual.

Green is the central colour of the spectrum, so it makes sense that it is associated with our most central chakra. Green has strong ties to healing and obviously nature. However, the Heart Chakra can also be represented as pink because of the relationship with love.

The Heart Chakra is linked to the thymus gland and immune system. It can have an impact on our lungs, breasts, arms, and hands, and most logically, our heart.

Physical symptoms when blocked: You might experience heart problems such as palpitations or in extreme cases, heart attacks. There may be links between high blood pressure and poor circulation. Some may experience respiratory problems while others can have stiff or painful joints in their hands.

Emotional symptoms when blocked: Heartbreak, extreme sadness, and even grief can be felt. Some people could be angry, jealous and feel hatred towards themselves and others.

An overactive Heart Chakra: People with an overactive Heart Chakra may be clinging in a relationship, they may not have set their own boundaries and have a tendency to try and please everyone.

An underactive Heart Chakra: It will be hard for you to be open about how you feel, and this can make you feel isolated from the world, even cold.

If your Heart Chakra is balanced, it will be easier for you to let go of the grudges you hold. Your emotions will flow freely, and you will not fear them but embrace them. It will be easier for you to trust people and form stronger relationships.

HEALING THROUGH SOUND

Mantras and affirmations will include the Bija mantra "Yam" and the English words "I love". Take the sounds and imagine pulling the energy up through your body. While I often like to imagine my chakras like the spinning firework wheel, in this case, as I chant, I like to see this energy as a river of love throughout me.

Suppose you want to practice some English affirmations. In that case, it is still important to imagine being filled with love, passion, and happiness.

- I am open to love
- I love myself unconditionally
- I am worthy of love
- I choose love
- I give love, I receive love
- My heart is filled with cheerfulness and joy

AWAKENING THE HEART CHAKRA WITH VISUALIZATION AND MEDITATION

When you hear Glastonbury, your mind will go straight to music, but it is a town that represents the idea of love and one of the Earth's Heart Chakras. As a dual chakra, the other location of the Heart Chakra is Shaftesbury (another town in the South of England. The towns fit together with Glastonbury a town of love and Shaftesbury one of will. Some believe the Heart Chakra expands to Stonehenge.

Interestingly, others feel that the Heart Chakra is the Halekalá volcano in Hawaii. The energy at the top of Halekalá emits the same frequency as the human heartbeat.

If you feel like your Heart Chakra is blocked or underactive, your visualisation needs to include imagining love flowing into your body. On the other hand, if your Heart Chakra is overactive, it's time to visualise this love flowing out of your body and sending it to others who need it.

Breathing is a vital part of meditation and the Heart Chakra because your lungs are one of the associated organs. When meditating, maintain your attention on deep breaths of green light. Each breath you take in should be directed to a pink light in the centre of your chest. See how the green light meets the pink as they swirl together.

You can also try Hridaya mudra. Sit down and bring the tips of your ring and middle finger to your thumb. Place your hands on your knees and concentrate on your heart and chest area. Your middle and ring fingers are associated with the energy channels of the heart. By bringing them to your thumb, you are essentially closing the circuit. Hridaya mudra can help you release the emotions that you have kept bottled up.

YOGA AND REIKI FOR YOUR HEART CHAKRA

Rather than putting your hand on your heart for Reiki, place it a little higher on your chest, between the Heart Chakra and the Throat Chakra. This is where your thymus gland is, and its job is to produce white blood cells that fight infections. Keep it there for a few minutes as your focus on your breathing.

The Marjaryasana/ Bitilasana (Cat/Cow Pose), Bhujangasana (Cobra Pose), and Ustrasana (Camel pose) are all lovely yoga poses that open the chest area to bring more energy to the Heart Chakra.

Cat/Cow pose- Position yourself on all fours. As you inhale, tuck your tummy right in and around your spine. On the exhale, you slowly roll your spine the other way so that you can feel your back dipping into the stretch. Repeat a few times with each inhale and exhale as deep as you can manage.

Cobra pose- Lie on your front, place your hands under your shoulders. Start by raising the crown of your head, then gradually elevate your upper body using your hands to support your body. Only lift up as far as it is comfortable.

Camel pose- Begin by kneeling on a mat and keep your hips in line with your knees. Reach behind you so that your shoulders drop and your chest opens. Hold your heels with your hands. If you struggle to hold both heels, start on your left side and then repeat with your left.

To encourage energy to the Heart Chakra through massage, you should focus on those muscles that are around the shoulders and very lightly on the pectoralis muscles, the large muscle across your chest. Remember, if you have any heart conditions, please consult a doctor first.

AROMATHERAPY AND CRYSTAL HEALING

Bergamot essential oil comes from the rind of the bergamot orange, which is actually green. It can help improve your mood and lower your cholesterol. Add fresh basil to your recipes to help lower the risk of heart disease, as well as cypress and eucalyptus essential oils.

There are lots of crystals that will help bring balance to your heart chakra. Emerald and green jade are the obvious choices for the colour but here are some of my other favourites:

Unakite Jasper- this lovely green crystal has soft touches of pink and one of nature's best crystals for the heart and the mind.

Pink Rhodochrosite- with its feminine energy, this crystal promotes commitment and caring. It can increase your feeling of self-worth and lift depression.

Rose Quartz- the crystal of universal love, unconditional love, self-love and friendships. It can bring about a sense of inner peace and help to restore trust in relationships.

Prehnite- this can be a lovely green colour and reminds me of grapes. It is another crystal associated with unconditional love and peace.

No one chakra is more important than the next, but personally, I noticed so many improvements in my life when I started creating balance in my Heart Chakra. It's about more than just feeling more love in a relationship. It's hard to see at times but there is so much love around us and when we are able to see this, life becomes more positive. The smaller things that used to get you down no longer seem as relevant.

AWAKENING THE THROAT CHAKRA

Located in the neck, the Throat Chakra or Vishuddha is imperative for our communication. It is also important because it is the gateway for energy to flow up to our head. Not only this, but the throat is where sounds are based on the rest of the body in the form of vibrations. Without the throat, we wouldn't be able to benefit as much from our bija sound mantras.

We most often visualise the Throat Chakra as blue, specifically turquoise blue but also aquamarine blue or even a cloudy purple.

The Throat Chakra is associated with the neck, the shoulders, ears and mouth. It can also impact the thyroid, a butterfly-shaped gland in front of the windpipe. It's what helps the body turn food into energy, our metabolism.

Physical symptoms when blocked: There may be a stiffness across your neck and shoulders. Sore throats can be expected or hoarseness. Some people suffer from laryngitis. When blocked, you may be susceptible to earaches and infections, problems with your teeth, or thyroid problems.

Emotional symptoms when blocked: People tend to be overly critical of themselves. There is a lot of fear when the Throat Chakra is blocked. But you might not be able to find the words to express this. It's quite normal also to feel insecure.

An overactive Throat Chakra: There is too much talking and not enough listening. Some people might become verbally abusive and look down on others.

An underactive Throat Chakra: You may feel overly shy. It could even be that you struggle to speak the truth and feel the need to lie.

You will be able to appreciate your wisdom when the Throat Chakra is balanced. You won't need to fear those moments when you know what you want to say but can't find the words to explain yourself. You can actively listen to others as well as your inner voice. You can express your feelings, your needs, and your creativity.

HEALING THROUGH SOUND

Our bija mantra is "Ham" but because of the importance of sound and vibrations, you may also want to use other Sanskrit mantras. I like the Adi Mantra, "Ong Namo Guru Dev Namo" (pronounced ong naa moo groo day na mo). It means "I bow to the creative energy of the infinitive; I bow to the divine channel of wisdom".

English affirmations can be linked to the words "I speak", for example:

- I speak the truth and I speak it freely
- My words express my love
- I share my creativity and wisdom
- I speak and I listen
- I am safe and I trust
- I communicate my truth

AWAKENING THE THROAT CHAKRA WITH VISUALIZATION AND MEDITATION

The Throat Chakra has three earthly locations. Two locations are in Egypt, Mount Sinai and the Great Pyramid of Giza. The third is the Mount of Olives in Jerusalem. If you look at the three locations on a map, you will be able to make out the connections in the form of a right triangle.

To attune to the planet Mercury and the energy of communication, close your eyes and breathe through your nose quickly for 20 seconds. Open your eyes and focus on one object while you maintain short rapid breaths. Close your eyes and repeat the process four or five times. This meditation is excellent for getting in touch with your creativity.

You can visualise a bright white light entering your body with each short breath, feel it pass down your throat and fill your lungs. This can be combined with a blue light passing in through your ears to help you listen. Each breath pulses the energy to your heart and into the blood to the rest of your body. Move your focus to the planet Mercury and visualise your ideas and dreams becoming a reality.

YOGA AND REIKI FOR YOUR THROAT CHAKRA

Naturally, you can massage your muscles that run the length of your neck to help release tension. If you want to have a little fun, try singing. The vibrations will spread throughout your body, and singing can help shy people find a bit of confidence. Sing wherever you feel comfortable doing so.

The same yoga poses we saw for the Heart Chakra can be used for the Throat Chakra. Once you are feeling more confident, balanced and stronger in your body, you can move on to the more advanced poses, such as the Salamba Sarvangasana (Supported Shoulder Stand), Halasana (Plow Pose), and Matsyasana (Fish Pose).

Supported Shoulder Stand- From lying flat on your back with your arms next to you, palms down, bring your knees up so that your feet are flat on the floor. Lift your hips off the floor and by using all of your core muscles, you will lift your knees towards your chest as your lower back comes up off the floor, followed by your mid-back. Use your hands to support your back. Straighten your legs so that your shoulders, hips and ankles are all in a straight line.

Plow Pose- Once you are balanced and breathing steadily in the shoulder stand, you can slowly bring one foot down to the floor behind your head. There should be no tension in your neck or shoulders. If this is comfortable, you can bring the other foot down. Don't be surprised if this takes a little practise.

Fish Pose- Lie down on the floor facing the ceiling. Tuck your hands under your bum and bring your index finger and thumbs together so that they form a diamond. You are going to gradually move your head so that the crown of your head is on the floor, you will be looking in the opposite direction of your feet. Open your chest towards the ceiling and take three or four slow deep breaths.

AROMATHERAPY AND CRYSTAL HEALING

Frankincense has a high spiritual frequency and has been shown to help with underactive thyroids. Geranium essential oil encourages communication with our inner selves and the sweetness of the citrus can also alleviate a sore throat. Peppermint is so refreshing I love it for everything. The sharpness of the essential oil has a positive impact on the sharpness of your mind and can help with respiratory infections.

The crystals for the Throat Chakra are some of my favourites because of the wide range of colours you can find. Rather than just looking at blue, explore the different shades of blue and those that have specks or streaks of white too.

Amazonite- It is more of a turquoise green and is good for creating emotional balance and to protect you from negativity.

Turquoise- depending on each stone, you might notice a stronger shade of blue. It's a good crystal to keep on you if you want to get better at expressing yourself clearly.

Lapis lazuli- It's a beautiful dark blue speckled stone. Along with improving clarity and creativity, it can not only help you to understand your inner truths but also express them.

Aquamarine- sometimes we need a little assistance being compassionate and understanding what others are telling us.

Aquamarine can help us overcome fears while allowing us to be more tolerant.

Emotional intelligence has become an incredibly important skill to have. Some of the smartest people I know are unable to explain some of their most basic emotions. Being able to communicate will allow us to experience more fulfilling lives, both personal and professional.

AWAKENING THE THIRD EYE CHAKRA

The Third Eye Chakra is the sixth chakra from the spine. It is located at the brow, above your nose and between your eyes. This chakra permits us to see the inner and outer worlds, more precisely, we can internalise the outer world and internalise the inner world. As it is located in the brain, when balanced, we can also experience a balance between the left and right hemispheres of the brain.

The Third Eye Chakra takes us one step closer to the spiritual world. Its energy can help us with our spiritual contemplation and self-reflection. Our eyes allow us to see the world and draw our own conclusions but the Third Eye lets us see the world from the point of view of an observer.

The Sanskrit name for the Third Eye Chakra is Ajna. It is associated with the colour blue, or a bluish-purple, even indigo. It can also be seen as translucent purple.

It is linked to the pituitary gland (the master gland), the eyes and the brow. This chakra is associated with the base of the skull and our biorhythms, the cycles that our body goes through like sleep.

Physical symptoms when blocked: Some of the most frequent problems are with vision, dizziness and headaches. It is even possible to experience migraines. Insomnia and other sleep disorders may also be symptoms.

Emotional symptoms when blocked: Through related to sleep disorders, you may suffer from nightmares. You may feel sceptical of everything or even extremely paranoid. Vivid dreams and delusions are also symptoms.

An overactive Third Eye Chakra: It may be impossible for you to focus or your mind easily drifts off. It can also be difficult for you to stay in touch with reality and your good judgement.

An underactive Third Eye Chakra: You might be stuck in the past and be scared of what is ahead. It's quite normal to be stuck in your ways of thinking and not be willing to explore new ideas. It is also possible that rather than trusting your inner voice, you stick to the rules of authority.

Balance in your Third Eye Chakra gives you the wisdom and the ability to see problems from a different perspective. It takes you that little step closer to enlightenment and even those who are sceptical of the spiritual world are more accepting of that which is beyond us. The sense of clarity that comes with a balanced Third Eye Chakra brings a whole new level of harmony to your world.

HEALING THROUGH SOUND

"Aum" is the bija mantra for the Third Eye Chakra, the source of all sound and the sound that will activate the energy in this chakra. The power of "Aum" is immense, so I often combine it with my English affirmations, which will be related to "I see".

Don't limit your affirmations to what you can physically see around you, it goes much deeper than that:

- I see each situation as an opportunity to grow
- I see and trust how my intuition guides me
- I am one with my higher power
- My third eye is all-seeing
- I welcome new experiences and new energy
- I believe in my imagination

AWAKENING THE THIRD EYE CHAKRA WITH VISUALIZATION AND MEDITATION

This chakra shifts locations with each new age, approximately every 2,100 to 2,500 years. Astrologers also believe that the Third Eye Chakra coordinates with constellations. Now, we are in the Age of Aquarius and so the location once again is in England, Glastonbury, specifically Glastonbury Tor. When we move into the Age of Capricorn, the Third Eye Chakra will be found in Brazil.

Saturn, in Kundalini, showers people with wealth. Some like to see this as material wealth. When I use visualisation, I imagine myself surrounded by rings like Saturn, though mine are blue and indigo. I feel the wealth of knowledge and the faith in myself spinning around me.

A blocked Third Eye Chakra can point to a restriction of your thought patterns. Regularly meditating will help to encourage your wisdom to flow and a stronger trust in your intuition. It is important to meditate with your eyes open. Only when your eyes are open can your third eye see your inner self. Imagine your consciousness looking through your eyes to the light inside your mind. Pressing the tip of your tongue to the roof of your mouth can stimulate the Third Eye Chakra from below. Breathe slowly through your nose.

YOGA AND REIKI FOR YOUR THIRD EYE CHAKRA

Massage can really help with headaches and migraines, particularly if you combine it with the right essential oils. Though you can massage your forehead, the bridge of your nose and around the ears, I like to work with a friend as it is much easier for them to massage the pressure points at the base of the skull.

You can also use your index finger to apply pressure on your Third Eye Chakra for one minute. Firm pressure can help to reduce eye strain, alleviate sinus pressure and help with headaches.

For yoga, you can work on Balasana (Child's Pose), Uttanasana (Standing Forward Fold), and Catur Svanasana (Dolphin Pose).

Child's Pose- I always get a sense of comfort from this pose. Sit on your heels and stretch your fingers forward in front of you on the mat. Extend your body as you rest your forehead on the floor in front of your knees and pull your arms behind you so that your hands are on either side of your feet.

Standing Forward Fold- Inhale as you bring your arms up in a circle, so your hands are above your head. On the exhale, fold down at the hips and reach your hands to the calf muscles, closer to the ankles if you can. You might need to start with your knees slightly bent until you build up your flexibility.

Dolphin Pose- Start on all fours, straighten your legs as you keep your forearms and palms flat on the ground. Keep your forearms flat and gently push your shoulder blades down. You should try to keep an even amount of weight on your feet and arms.

AROMATHERAPY AND CRYSTAL HEALING

I do always try to use each plant to the maximum, bay laurel is great to throw whole leaves into soups and stews. As an essential oil, it can increase your awareness and perception. It can stimulate both the left and right hemispheres of the brain. Palo Santo is often burned and used for cleansing. It's a lovely sweet smell and can enhance your spiritual awareness. Lavender is the right colour for the Third Eye Chakra and its ability to help you relax will assist with meditation.

As with mantras, it is your intention that is most important with healing crystals. The following are well known for their ability to help balance your Third Eye Chakra, but you can use others.

Amethyst- you can find this crystal in dark to light shades of purple. It is used to stimulate the chakra and create balance. It can offer you wisdom and protection from harm.

Black Obsidian- as well as emotional balance, black obsidian can remove negativity.

Purple Fluorite- some call this crystal the dream crystal and can help those who suffer from nightmares and spiritual discomfort. It can make decision making easier and improve our confidence.

Clear Quartz- with a focus on the Third Eye Chakra, the powerful vibrational energy of Clear Quartz can help transmit your thoughts to the rest of the universe.

Our chakra learning will soon be coming to an end, but if you are the type of person who loves to learn and explore, it certainly doesn't mean that chakra healing is almost over. The final chapter will look at the Crown Chakra.

AWAKENING THE CROWN CHAKRA

The name comes from the idea that the Crown Chakra sits on the top of our head. Even though it is furthest from our Root Chakra it has strong ties because they are both extremes. The Root Chakra keeps us grounded, whereas the Crown Chakra is associated with an awareness of our higher consciousness. In Sanskrit, it is called Sahasrara.

As the location suggests, this chakra is the closest link to the divine. For those who are religious, they will be able to appreciate a closer connection to their god. For those who aren't they will still gain from the uttermost clarity. Unblocking and finding balance in your Crown Chakra releases you from your limitations, in space and time.

We associate the Crown Chakra with the colour purple or violet. That being said, the sheer power of the Crown Chakra can also have ties to gold, white, and a clear bright light.

With regards to our body, the Crown Chakra is linked to our pituitary and pineal glands and the central nervous system. With regards to our brain, it can be associated with the hypothalamus and cerebral cortex.

Physical symptoms of a blocked Crown Chakra: Mental fog and confusion are often seen with a blocked Crown Chakra. There could be neurological disorders or mental disorders like schizophrenia. Some may experience nerve pain.

Emotional symptoms of a blocked Crown Chakra: You may be feeling particularly lonely with no direction in your life. It's not just that you don't have spiritual guidance, you might feel like you don't deserve it. Some people become overly attached to material objects.

An overactive Crown Chakra: there is such a thing as an addiction to spirituality or reckless behaviour when it comes to your bodily needs. It could be difficult for you to control your feelings.

An underactive Crown Chakra: If you find setting goals and reaching them a challenge, your Crown Chakra could be underactive. It's also likely that you aren't open to the concept of spirituality.

When you start to recognise your spiritual side and open your mind to all that is sacred, you will know that your Crown

Chakra is starting to become balanced. The best way to describe a Crown Chakra that is flowing with the right energy is a state of bliss, ecstasy and pure happiness.

HEALING THROUGH SOUND

"Om" refers to Atman and Braham, the soul and the entirety of the universe or the supreme spirit respectively. It can be used alone or as part of longer mantras, for example, "Om Santi, Santi Om".

In English, we use the words "I am", which leaves you a great deal of freedom to create your own meaningful affirmations. Here is some inspiration:

- I am at peace
- I am light
- I am divine
- I go beyond my limiting beliefs
- I am infinite
- I am complete

AWAKENING THE CROWN CHAKRA WITH VISUALISATION AND MEDITATION

You might assume that Mount Everest would be the earth's Crown Chakra due to its height. In fact, while still in the Himalayas, it is Mount Kailash that is dubbed as the "roof of the world". Though approximately 7,000 ft higher, Everest doesn't have the same sacredness as Mount Kailash. It is considered the most sacred mountain in Tibet and many consider it offensive to climb it due to it being so holy.

Jupiter is the planet associated with the Crown Chakra. It is one of the most effective in the birth charts and is highly spiritual. In astrology, Jupiter is the teacher of the science of light and the ruler of the Sun and the Moon. The planet Jupiter is the fourth brightest object in the sky. This brightness can help us with our visualisation. Such light and brightness can be drawn in and absorbed, the power of the light reaching every inch of us.

When we meditate, it is helpful to relax our head and face, even imagine your head as a floating lotus surrounded by water. With each breath you take, imagine the lotus opening just that little bit more. The purple light that radiates from your head should be seen growing in a beam towards the sky. At the end of your meditation, be thankful, whether that is to the divine or your higher self.

YOGA AND REIKI FOR YOUR CROWN CHAKRA

For Reiki healing by yourself, you should aim to place the palms of your hands on the back of your head with your wrists covering the crown of your head. Massages general focus on the scalp, perhaps the reason why I am often tempted to pay my children to brush my hair!

Run your fingers through your hair a few times, just gently scraping the scalp with your fingertips but not your nails. Now start to massage your scalp with your fingertips in circular motions. Don't feel that you have to massage each area methodically. Instead, have faith in your body and let your instincts guide your fingers. Also, don't feel the need for these head massaging tools. As funky as they seem, your hands are the best healing tools. You can also use your affirmations and visualise a purple light around each area you massage.

Paschimottanasana (Seated Forward Bend), Adho Mukha Sukhasana (Easy Pose with Forward Fold) and Shavasana (Corpse Pose) will allow you to feel the peace and serenity while the Crown Chakra becomes more balanced.

Seated Forward Bend- You will start by sitting up straight with your legs nicely stretched out in front of you. Raise your hands in a circular motion up above your head as you breathe in. Slowly exhale and allow your body to fold towards your legs. You may find that in the beginning, your hands will reach your knees or your shins. Don't panic, if you do this pose each day you will soon be able to hold your ankles as you feel the stretch along your spine.

Easy Pose with Forward Fold- Sit up nice and tall and cross each leg as you bend your knees. Each foot should rest on the opposite knee. Inhale as you stretch your arms above your head and fold forward on the exhale. Lower your head towards your knees and place your hands on your mat in front of you.

You will feel the stretch along your thighs but don't push your-self further than you can.

Corpse Pose- it might look like you are just lying on the floor but pay attention to pulling your shoulder blades slightly together underneath you and lift your chin upwards a touch. This pose requires deep breathing and each exhale should allow your body to sink a little more towards the floor. This is a great way to start your day, even from your bed.

AROMATHERAPY AND CRYSTAL HEALING

A lot of the essential oils we have already seen can also be used for the Crown Chakra, such as Lavender, Jasmine, and Frankin-cense. You can also try Vetiver. This essential oil can help you to remember your vivid dreams, sometimes signs of what our subconscious wants. Helichrysum has a high spiritual frequency and may help to reduce the strength of headaches and migraines. Spikenard will help you to find your emotional balance, enjoy a more restful sleep and assist your meditation.

The same can be said with our crystals. There is no need to go out and buy more if you already have a good selection of crys-tals. Nevertheless, if you are on the lookout for more, you might want to consider:

Selenite- The white stone can enable a better connection with the divine and with the high vibrations can also be used for cleansing and creating a calming space.

Clear Quartz- This is more transparent than Selenite. It may help soothe pain in your nerves. Generally, it will help to harmonise the 7 chakras.

Charoite- I am a real fan of the white, lavender and pearly lustre of this stone. As well as opening the Heart Chakra, it is considered to be the stone of service and altruism.

Diamond- The pure white of diamond can awaken your crown chakra and bring you greater awareness. It is a symbol of purity and love, positivity and strength.

Some people might understandably yet mistakenly see the Crown Chakra as the end of the line, maybe more so if they aren't religious. Others see this as the holy grail of chakras. Remember that the goal is to awaken each of the chakras so that the right quantity and quality of energy is flowing through our bodies. It's a process, a pleasant, eye-opening and enjoyable one that can't be rushed so that we can reach the Crown Chakra and a higher state of being. Take your time. The changes we make as we balance our chakras will last a lifetime, it's not a sprint!

CONCLUSION

A friend of mine wanted me to check her chakra healing kit that she had bought. There was a new yoga mat, there were at least 10 crystals, a jewellery making kit, mala beads and more essential oils than the local pharmacy. Before we wrap up this book on modern chakras, please remember that while all of these tools can enhance the healing process, they are also not compulsory. You need your body and your mind to awaken your chakras. People get it the wrong way around and think that by popping a crystal in their pocket they will start to see improvements in their life. We need intention.

It is necessary to begin our healing process by understanding exactly what is wrong, whether the symptoms are physical, emotional, or both. Not everyone will have symptoms that are associated with just one chakra. It's possible to have lower backache, anger issues, and a weak immune system. While the first part of this book introduces you to chakras, the final chapters will have helped you to identify your blocked chakras.

It is normal to feel slightly overwhelmed in the beginning. I remember almost feeling scared that I was going to get it wrong. By using the techniques in this book, you can't get it wrong. There is no technique or combination of techniques that will cause you to suffer. This is the main reason why I have stayed far away from the topic of opening chakras, as this runs a risk of 'too much too soon'.

The emotional journey of balancing your chakras can bring up a whole range of feelings that you might have even forgotten you had. On occasions, it might feel like there are some highs and lows as you work through each of these emotions. Keep your focus on the end goal and remember that though there may be difficult moments, you should celebrate this experience.

My other piece of advice from experience is not to try too many techniques at once. You might think that the best results are going to come about when you have your essential oils, crystal circle, ocean waves playing in the background and so on, but if you are new to meditation and visualisation, this might be distracting. To master skills like meditation and visualisation, I think it's better to start simple. Go and sit in a field or lay in your garden. Not all of the chakra techniques have to be done at the same time. Play around with aromatherapy, massage, the crystals, and even the mantras until you start to feel that you are gaining from each part of the healing.

Needless to say, I am not a doctor. Everything in this book is completely natural but that doesn't mean to say the alternative medicine can be used with the current medication you are taking. Please check with your physician if you have any doubts. The same is said for those who are pregnant, check with your midwife first. We are all different and have different conditions so to be on the safe side, just ask before you try.

I am convinced that no matter what gender, size, or age you are, yoga is going to become your new best friend. Yoga is easy to include in your daily routine and just 5 or 10 minutes before you start your day can really boost your mood. If you are unsure of any of the positions or that you are getting them right, it would be wise to sign up for a few classes, even if it's just until you start to feel a little bit more confident. Again, pregnant ladies and those with medical conditions, please check with your doctor first.

As you begin to feel the energy flow up through your body, take some time to stop and look around. Reassess your goals so that you are continuing to strive for new things but don't forget to be grateful for what you have at this moment.

Back in the 90s, I went to Glastonbury, the festival and the town. You do notice something special there. To say you feel the love might sound a little hippy, but you can. It's a positive place where people smile, they are polite and genuinely happy. I have also been lucky enough to go to Lake Titicaca and Mount Kailash. It's impossible to describe the raw beauty these locations have. A beauty so pure that it translates into power. Each breath of air in these majestical places fills you with power and peace.

My visit to Lake Titicaca was before I had learnt about the Earth's chakras. Once I put the pieces of the puzzle together, I had one of those moments "That's why I felt so good there!". One of my goals is to visit all 7 and if you ever get the opportunity even to visit one, take it. Don't worry about your mantras, your crystals, or your yoga mat. Just get the best view, sit down, and be present in that moment.

If I had to leave a final message it would be to explore your chakras. Learn what works for you and what can be saved for a different time in your life. Don't be afraid to try new things and delve into concepts that you haven't uncovered yet. Just because you haven't experienced a higher connection yet, doesn't mean it isn't there waiting for you.

Coming to the end of a book I often feel a little sad, like I am going to miss writing to you. On the other hand, I can be excited because I can begin my next project. If you have enjoyed this book, then a happy review on Amazon would be so appreciated!! You can also have a look for my book Healing Mantras if you want to learn more about the ancient Hindu practice of healing through sound vibrations. Good luck with your journey, I know you are going to excel!

Thank you for reading my book. If you have enjoyed reading it perhaps you would like to leave a star rating and a review for me on Amazon? It really helps support writers like myself create more books. You can leave a review for me by scanning the QR code below:

Thank you so much. Verda Harper

REFERENCES

B. (2020, February 26). Everything to Know About Earth Chakras, and How to Heal Through Them. Retrieved from https://www.bemytravelmuse.com/healing-earth-chakras/

Bear, Y. (2017, July 30). Balance Your Sacral Chakra with these Yoga Poses. Retrieved from https://www.rte.ie/lifestyle/living/2017/0727/893438-balance-your-sacral-chakra-with-these-yoga-poses/

Benton, E. (2019, March 27). Kundalini Yoga: Everything You Need to Know. Retrieved from https://www.prevention.com/fitness/workouts/a26907922/kundalini-yoga/

Cirino, E. (2018, December 4). Reflexology 101. Retrieved from https://www.healthline.com/health/what-is-reflexology#safety

Clalit Health Services. (2018, January 25). Effects of Brief Guided Imagery for Chronic Pain in Patients Diagnosed With Fibromyalgia - Full Text View - ClinicalTrials.gov. Retrieved from https://clinicaltrials.gov/ct2/show/NCT02846194

Cultural Chakras. (2019, November 8). Retrieved from https://www.bearmckay.com/blog/cultural-chakras

HeereJawharat.com. (2015, June 1). Jupiter Nature. Retrieved from https://www.heerejawharat.com/astrology/planets-significance/brihaspati-jupitar.php

Hillary on HubPages. (2011). Retrieved from https://hubpages.com/@greenlotus

History of Yoga. (2020, June 11). Retrieved from https://www.yogabasics.com/learn/history-of-yoga/

Houston, D. (2020, April 29). How To Program Crystals. Retrieved from https://meanings.crystalsandjewelry.com/how-to-program-crystals/

How To Heal Your Body & Mind With Reflexology. (2020, September 2). Retrieved from https://thewhoot.com/health/reflexology

Inam, H. (2019, December 3). What are affirmations and how to affirm yourself? - Broftware Labs. Retrieved from https://medium.com/broftware-labs/what-are-affirmations-and-how-to-affirm-yourself-e079500c732c

Jeffrey, S. (2020, August 28). How to Ground Yourself | 9 Powerful Grounding Techniques. Retrieved from https://scottjeffrey.com/how-to-ground-yourself/

Kundalini Yoga - Key Mantras. (n.d.). Retrieved from https://www.kundaliniyoga.org/Mantras

L. (2019a, November 26). Guide To The Chakras For Beginners And Healing Practitioners. Retrieved from https://www.chakras.info

L. (2019b, December 4). Understanding The 12 Chakras And What They Mean. Retrieved from https://www.chakras.info/12-chakras/

L. (2019c, December 5). What To Do When Your Crown Chakra Is Blocked. Retrieved from https://www.chakras.info/blocked-crown-chakra/

Marfan Syndrome | Hartford HealthCare. (n.d.). Retrieved from https://hartfordhealthcare.org/services/heart-vascular/conditions/marfan-syndrome

McGinley, K. (2020, August 12). 7 Chakra Meditations to Keep You in Balance. Retrieved from https://chopra.com/articles/7-chakra-meditations-to-keep-you-in-balance

mindbodygreen. (2020a, January 30). The Transformative Powers of "Bija Mantra" Meditation. Retrieved from https://www.mindbodygreen.com/0-5930/The-Transformative-Powers-of-Bija-Mantra-Meditation.html mindbodygreen. (2020b, April 21). Kundalini Yoga 101: Everything You Wanted To Know. Retrieved from https://www.mindbodygreen.com/articles/kundalini-yoga-101-everything-you-wanted-to-know

Moon, H. (2019, December 23). Crystal Vibration Numbers Made Simple. Retrieved from https://hibiscusmooncrystalacademy.com/crystal-vibrations/

Provisions, G. (2018, July 18). Open your Crown & Third Eye Chakras with Head Massage. Retrieved from https://blog.goddessprovisions.com/crown-chakra-massage/

Rataic, T. (2020, March 3). Your Heart Chakra: 5 Quick + Easy Tips to Heal Your Center of Love + Compassion. Retrieved from https://thereikiguide.com/your-heart-chakra-5-quick-and-easy-tips-to-heal-your-center-of-love-and-compassion/

Science Wire from the Exploratorium and Public Radio International. (n.d.). Retrieved from https://www.exploratorium.edu/theworld/sonar/trythis.html

Sehra, N. (2018, September 10). Use These 7 Mantras to Clear Your Throat Chakra and Speak Your Truth. Retrieved from https://www.yogiapproved.com/om/throat-chakra-healing-mantras/

studio2108. (2013, March 26). What is the origin of the chakra system? – Indigo Massage & Wellness. Retrieved from https://

indigomassagetherapy.com/uncategorized/what-is-the-origin-of-the-chakra-system/

Terrell, J. (n.d.). Awakening You Chakras (Energy Centers). Retrieved from https://www.awakenment-wellness.com/chakras.html

The Importance of Visualization in Sports. (n.d.). Retrieved from https://www.peaksports.com/sports-psychology-blog/sports-visualization-athletes/

What are Affirmations? (n.d.). Retrieved from http://powerthoughtsmeditationclub.com/what-are-affirmations/

What is Reiki? (2019, September 11). Retrieved from https://www.reiki.org/faqs/what-reiki

YJ Editors. (2018, December 4). How to Use the Seven Chakras in Your Yoga Practice. Retrieved from https://www.yogajournal.com/yoga-101/a-guide-to-the-chakras